NO TEARS FOR
ERNEST CREECH

NO TEARS FOR
ERNEST CREECH
The death of a coal miner in the hills of Appalachian

LORETTA CREECH AND
ANNETTE CREECH FRANCK

ReadersMagnet, LLC

Table of Contents

FORM KSP-2

SUPPLEMENTARY REPORT

KENTUCKY STATE POLICE

Case No. 13-4924

Radio No.

Name of Complainant   COMM. ATTY., BURNS, LESTER

Nature Request or Complaint   WILLFUL MURDER

Officers Report:

INVESTIGATION:

At 1622 Hours on Wednesday March 3, 1965, EARL FOREST, Supt. Leatherwood #1 Mine Leatherwood, Kentucky called and reported that one of his foremen, COY BLAIR, had called him and advised that an employee had been shot and killed at Leatherwood, Kentucky. The call was taken by 1st Sgt. WILLARD MITCHELL, who proceeded to the scene accompanied by Trooper PAUL G. RUSSELL and Trooper GERALD ARCHER.

Detectives J. E. Combs and E. E. Wilcox along with the Leslie County Coroner, DWAYNE WALKER, arrived on the scene at about 1800 Hours. The victim, ERNEST CREECH, apparently had not been moved. He had been sitting under the steering wheel of a 1950 International Pickup Truck color cream with rust spots, bearing 1965 Kentucky license T148-542, and had slumped over on his right side his head toward the right side of the cab. He was dressed in coveralls which were soaked with blood.

The truck was sitting on right side of Ky 699, headed Northwest. The rear of the truck was about 132' NW of Perry and Leslie County line post, in Leslie County.

A single bullet hole (about .30 Cal in size) was observed in the rear of the cab, in the metal, about 8" above the top of the bed and about 6" under the bottom left corner of the rear window, slightly to the left of the glass and was about 52" from the ground. The bullet traveled throug two pieces of metal of the cab, entered the back of the victim, made exit at front of left arm pit, proceeded on and struck the steering wheel near spoke joint and on to dash striking metal over instrument pannel which was not penetrated. (see diagram)

The left half of the two piece rear window, had been struck by two missiles of sometype which shattered the glass but didnot penetrate.

The left door glass was down except for about 6" of glass and near the top center, it appeared to have been struck and shattered slightly.

The angle at which the bullet struck the truck, indicated that it had came from the area where the pickets were congregated around fire Barrels. (See Diagram attached)

It was learned that two men, BENTLY BOGGS and CARL BOGGS were inthe truck with ERNEST CREECH at the time the shot

March 6, 1965

Date

Report Reviewed by

Det. E. E. Wilcox   U179

Officer Making Report

FORM KSP-2

SUPPLEMENTARY REPORT
KENTUCKY STATE POLICE

Case No. 13-4924

Radio No. _____

Name of Complainant   COMM. ATTY. BURNS, LESTER

Nature Request or Complaint   WILLFUL MURDER

Officers Report:

INVESTIGATION CONTINUED:

was fired. (Statement attached).
BENTLY BOGGS later added in addition to his statement that:
"I saw Junior GAYHART put a gun back into his truck. I heard
GRANT BAKER YELL: "Take the God Damn son of a bitch out of
here"."." This statement was made to Trooper PAUL G. RUSSELL.

Junior GAYHART was picked up by Sgt. JACKIE MURPHY and Deputy
Sheriff EDWARD FARLER. He denied having any gun other than
a .22 Cal Pistol.

The scene was photographed and the body was removed to the
Maggard Funeral Home in Hazard, Kentucky, and the truck was
towed to HORTONS garage in Hyden, Kentucky. A search at the
scene failed to find any fragment of bullet.

JIM BAKER of Cutshin, Kentucky was contacted at his home by
coroner DWAYNE WALKER and Det. E. E. WILCOX. He admitted that
he was on the scene, but denied any knowledge as to who had
fired the shot. He stated that he saw a gun barrel sticking
out the window on the drivers side of the victims truck and
that he hit the ditch. He stated that he heard one shot but
didnot know from which it came. He denied that he had saw any
gun in the possession of any of the pickets.

The Commonwealth Attorney LESTER BURNS arrived on the scene
and ordered that all Pickets who could be identified as having
been on the scene at the time the shot was fired be arrested.
Attorney LESTER BURNS then contacted Leslie County Circuit
Judge BILLIE DIXON, who approved.

A total of 15 men were arrested and taken to the Leslie County
Court House where they were questioned by Atty BURNS and their
statements taken in affidavits.

Twelve were held, charged with Murder and aiding and abetting
Murder and three were released.

Atty LESTER BURNS advised that he will seek Murder Indictments
by the Leslie County Grand Jury on Monday March 8, 1965.

DISPOSITION OF CASE:

INVESTIGATION CONTINUED

March 6, 1965

Date

Report Reviewed by

Det. E. E. Wilcox   U179

Officer Making Report

Victim: CREECH, ERNEST a WM DOB 12-3-26
Killed on March 3, 1965 at about 1610 Hours

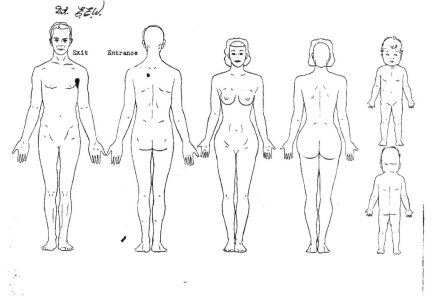

FORM KSP 1
REV. 7-1-60

CASE REPORT
KENTUCKY STATE POLICE

CASE NO. 13-4924

RADIO NO.

BUSINESS PHONE 436-2433

REPORTED BY **FOREST, EARL**

HOME PHONE 675-3571

ADDRESS **Leatherwood, Kentucky**

NATURE REQUEST OR COMPLAINT		DATE	TIME	HOW RECEIVED		
WILLFUL MURDER		3/3/65	1610 Hrs	Phone		
EXACT LOCATION ☒ RURAL ☐ URBAN		CITY		COUNTY		STATE
Ky 699 Leslie & Perry County Line		Leatherwood		Leslie		Kentucky
RECEIVED BY	UNIT NO.	DATE	TIME	REPORT REVIEWED BY		
1st Sgt. WILLARD MITCHELL	114	3/3/65	1622 Hrs			
ASSIGNED TO	UNIT NO.	DATE	TIME	BY		REPORT DUE
Post #13 Units		3/3/65	1700 Hrs	Sgt. Mitchell		ASAP.

INITIAL REPORT: IN DETAIL

EARL FOREST, SUPERINTENDENT Leatherwood #1 Mine, called and reported that he had received a call from one of his foremen, who advised that an employee had been shot and killed near the Perry and Leslie County line on Kentucky Highway 699.

Officers dispatched to the Scene were: 1st Sgt. WILLARD MITCHELL, Troopers PAUL RUSSEL and GERALD ARCHER, Sgt. Jackie MURPHY, Detectives J. E. COMBS and E. E. WILCOX.

3/4/65		1st Willard Mitchell	U 114.
DATE	REPORT REVIEWED BY	OFFICER MAKING REPORT	UNIT NO.

X

FORM KSP-2

SUPPLEMENTARY REPORT
KENTUCKY STATE POLICE

Case No. 13-4924

Radio No. _____

Name of Complainant BURNS, LESTER, Manchester, Ky.

Nature Request or Complaint   MURDER

Officers Report: BANKS, Sgt. Sam

INVESTIGATION: On Wednesday, March 3, 1965, at 2145 hours,
the writer and Trooper M. J. HARRISON received
a radio message from Post 10 radio advising
a warrant charging accessory to Murder against
Bill BAKER of Big Laurel, Kentucky, a W/M,
DOB: 7-27-16, (48), 5'11", 200 lbs., Brown
hair, Blue eyes.

The accused BAKER, was arrested on the above
information by Sgt. BANKS and Trooper HARRISON
and was transported to Leslie County Court
House at Hyden, Kentucky, where he was released
to Sgt. Willard MITCHELL.

DISPOSITION: CASE PENDING

March 4, 1965
Date

Report Reviewed by

Sam Banks, Sgt.
Officer Making Report

RECORD OF SEIZED OR

RECOVERED   PROPERTY

SEIZED X

RECOVERED

DELIVERED BY

FROM WHOM   Taken from Truck of Victim Ernest Creech

CASE NO.   13-4924

DATE   3/3/   19 65

POST NO.   13

Item No.	No. of Items	Description	Serial No.	Value
1	1	Model 50 12Ga Winchester Semi-Auto Shotgun full choke with shell belt and 10 shells	112609	$50.00

THE ABOVE LISTED ARTICLE RECEIVED AND CHECKED AS LISTED.

Signed   Det. E. E. Wilcox 175
Responsible Officer

Date   2/16/66

THIS IS TO CERTIFY THAT ON THIS DATE I HAVE RECEIVED FROM THE KENTUCKY STATE POLICE THE LISTED PROPERTY AND HEREBY RELEASE THEM FROM ALL RESPONSIBILITY CONCERNING THIS PROPERTY.

KSP Form 41
Revised 1-1-65

Signed   Gladys Creech
Address
in full   Bonnyman, Ky.

xii

KENTUCKY STATE POLICE
RECORD OF SEIZED OR
RECOVERED PROPERTY

SEIZED   X

RECOVERED

DELIVERED BY

FROM WHOM   From Truck of Victim ERNEST CREECH

CASE NO. 13-4924

DATE 3/3/   19 65

POST NO.   13

Item No.	No. of Items	Description	Serial No.	Value
1	1	Model 94 Lever Action Winchester 30-30 Cal. (New) Serial 2824880 with one box of 20 cartridges	2824880	$60.00

THE ABOVE LISTED ARTICLE RECEIVED AND CHECKED AS LISTED.

Signed _Everett E. Wilcox_
Responsible Officer

Date   3-25-64

THIS IS TO CERTIFY THAT ON THIS DATE I HAVE RECEIVED FROM THE KENTUCKY STATE POLICE THE LISTED PROPERTY AND HEREBY RELEASE THEM FROM ALL RESPONSIBILITY CONCERNING THIS PROPERTY.

KSP Form 41
Revised 1-1-65

Signed _Earl Faust_
Address
in full _Blue Diamond Co_
Leatherwood

SUPPLEMENTARY REPORT
KENTUCKY STATE POLICE

Case No. 13-4924

Radio No. _____

Name of Complainant Comm Atty BURNS, LESTER

Nature Request or Complaint   WILFULL MURDER

Officers Report:

OFFENSE:	WILFULL MURDER
DATE AND TIME:	Wednesday March 3, 1965 at about 1610 Hours
WEATHER CONDITION:	Clear and Dry
REPORTED BY:	BLAIR, COY Tilford, Kentucky Phone: 675-3513
PLACE:	This offense occurred on Kentucky Highway 699, about 132 Feet West of the Perry and Leslie County line and further, 15 Feet East of the junction of Ky 699 and Kentucky 221 in Leslie County. The Victim was sitting on the left side of a 1950 International Pickup Truck behind the steering wheel when the fatal shot was fired.
COMPLAINANT:	BURNS, LESTER H. Commonwealth Attorney 41st Judicial District, Manchester, Kentucky. Phone: 598-2723.
VICTIM:	CREECH, ERNEST a WM DOB December 3, 1926, 5'5", 145, Brown hair, Blue Eyes. Address: Bonnyman, Kentucky. Occupation: Coal Miner.
MOTIVE:	Probably the result of a Labor Disput. The Victim had been crossing a Picket line traveling to and from work at a Coal Mine which was being picketed.
MODUS OPERANDI:	On the morning of March 3, 1965, as CREECH, ERNEST, BOGGS, BENTLY and BOGGS, CARL were going to work, a missle of some type was thrown at this same truck as it passed the Picket line, shattering a small portion of the rear window.
	On the afternoon of March 3, 1965, as this truck traveled passed the Picket line, an object is alledged to have been thrown which struck the rear of the cab. The operator of the truck, CREECH, ERNEST, stopped the truck and according to one of the occupants, stuck a 30-30 Cal rifle out the left window. He had apparently pulled the barrel of the rifle back into the truck when the fatal shot was fired. The angle of the path of the bullet indicated that it came from the direction of a fire barrel around which the pickets were congreated.
ACCUSED:	See Attached
RELATIVES:	" "

3/4/65

Date

Report Reviewed by

Det. E. E. Wilcox   U179

Officer Making Report

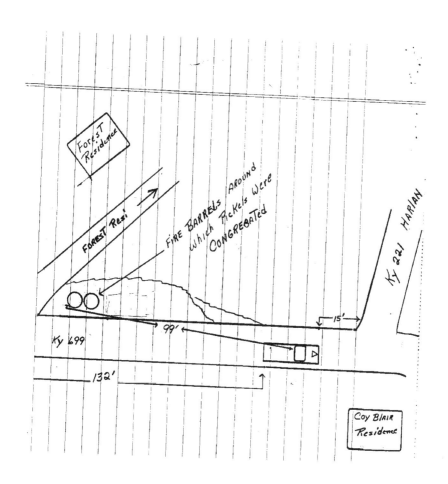

SUPPLEMENTARY REPORT
KENTUCKY STATE POLICE

Case No. 13-4924

Radio No. _____

Name of
Complainant __COMM ATTY BURNS, LESTER_____

Nature Request
or Complaint____ WILFULL MURDER

Officers Report:

(Statement of CARL and BENTLY BOGGS)
Passengers in truck with the Victim , made to Trooper PAUL RUSSELL

(Bently Boggs)
"We were coming from work at Leatherwood #1 Mine and had stopped
on top of the hill and started out onto Ky 699 heading toward
Wooton, Kentucky.

Something was thrown at the truck as we pulled onto Ky 699 and hit
the back of the cab. Ernest Creech, the driver, stopped and looked
back. We all looked back at the picket line. We saw everyman in their
cars had guns pointed at us and some started walking toward us and at
this point, someone fired a shot hitting the back of the cab hitting
in the back. As soon as Creech was hit, I, Bently Boggs got out of
the truck as I was sitting on the outside, the outside passenger,
I went around toward the driver side, I told the pickets: "Boys
let me take this boy to the Hospital". They said: "Take the God
Damn son of a bitch out of here and don't bring him back."

About this time, Coy Blair, who lives beside the Highway and is a
foreman at the mine, called to me not to move the truck. I went to
Coy's house and called or had Coy to call the State Police.

I(Carl Boggs) was sitting in the middle and everything happened as
Bently stated only when Ernest stopped, he reached for his rifle
and started the barrel out the window and got the barrel half out the
window and I begged him to put it back into the truck. He did and as
he got it back in the truck, he was shot. We both got out and Bently
went to call the Police and Ambulance. None of the pickets came about
the truck and one, a Chev Pickup left and went toward Harlan County
and gone about 15 minutes and came back and parked back in the picket
line. The pickets stayed around about 25 or 30 minutes and they left

(Bently Boggs) "I am sure the shot was not fired from the left side o
the road as I looked back in that direction. I am sure it came from
the direction of the fire."

We, BENTLY BOGGS and CARL BOGGS, have read the foregoing statement
and it is true and correct to the best of our knowledge.

S/Carl Boggs
Bently Boggs

March 4, 1965
Date

Report Reviewed by

Det. E. E. Wilcox   U179
Officer Making Report

FORM KSP-2

SUPPLEMENTARY REPORT
KENTUCKY STATE POLICE

Case No. 13-4924

Radio No. _____

Name of
Complainant __COMM ATTY BURNS, LESTER__   Nature Request
or Complaint _____

Officers Report:

INVESTIGATION
CONTINUED:

The following individuals were interviewed by Sgt. MURPHY
Trooper HOWARD and Comm. Atty. LESTER BURNS, but were not
arrested at the time.

BOWLING, BOONE a WM Address Cornettsville, Kentucky
CAUDILL, FRAUD a WM Fusonia, Kentucky
PRATT, DENNY VERNON a WM Cornettsville, Kentucky

They were later indicted by the Grand Jury and turned
themselves into the Leslie County Sheriff LAWRENCE HOWARD,
filled bond and were released.

BILL PERKINS Broadway St. Hazard, Kentucky, was also
indicted. He turned himself into the Sheriff, filled bond
and was released.

LOUIS SHEPHERD was interviewed by Comm Atty., but was not
charged at the time; However, he was later indicted by
the Grand Jury but due to his confinement to the Hospital,
has not been arrested.

The following individuals were arrested and no indictments
were returned against them: They were released after
being interviewed by Commonwealth Atty Burns.
HENSLEY, EUGENE Smilax, Kentucky
CHILDERS, JACK Big Fork, Kentucky
BAKER, GRANT Cutshin, Kentucky
BAKER, BILL Big Laurel, Kentucky
BAKER, JAMES B. Cutshin, Kentucky

DISPOSITION OF
CASE:

Investigation Continued

Attachments:

15 Sets fingerprints
14 Arrest Cards
1 Arrest Card forwarded in by KSP Harlan

4 INV 7's with information available on those who
surrendered to Sheriff Lawrence Howard.

15 sets prints
3-15-65

3/11/65
Date _____   Report Reviewed by _____   _E. E. Wilcox_
Officer Making Report

SUPPLEMENTARY REPORT
KENTUCKY STATE POLICE

Case No. 13-4924

Radio No. _____

Name of Complainant COMM ATTY., BURNS, LESTER

Nature Request or Complaint WILLFUL MURDER

Officers Report:

INVESTIGATION
CONTINUED:

On Friday March 5, 1965, Lt. BILLIE LYKINS, SGT. WILLAR
MITCHELL and Det. E. E. WILCOX again searched the victi
truck for the fatal bullet and sifted the debris on the
floor through a screen. The bullet was not found.

Later on the 5th of March, two students of the Hyden
Vocational School found a piece of lead in the truck
and turned it in at the Leslie County Sheriff's
Office. The students were: JULIAS W. RECORD and
WAYNE MURPHY.

The lead is stained with a substance appearing to
be blood and is battered beyond recognition as a
bullet; However, it is believed to be a .303 or
30-06 Calibre bullet from which the copper jacket
has been shed.

March 9, 1965

Date

Report Reviewed by

Det. E. E. Wilcox / U179

Officer Making Report

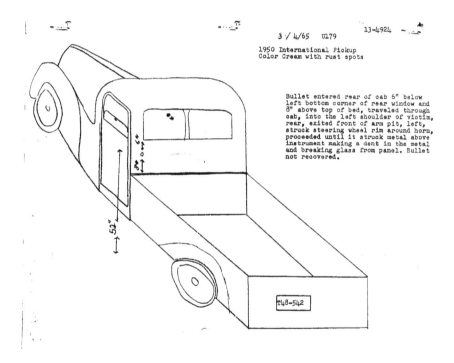

3 / 4/65   U179   13-4924

1950 International Pickup
Color Cream with rust spots

Bullet entered rear of cab 6" below
left bottom corner of rear window and
8" above top of bed, traveled through
cab, into the left shoulder of victim,
rear, exited front of arm pit, left,
struck steering wheel rim around horn,
proceeded until it struck metal above
instrument making a dent in the metal
and breaking glass from panel. Bullet
not recovered.

T48-542

FORM KSP-2

SUPPLEMENTARY REPORT
KENTUCKY STATE POLICE

Case No. 13-4924

Radio No. _____

Name of Complainant: Comm., Atty., BURNS, LESTER   Nature Request or Complaint: WILLFUL MURDER

Officers Report:

On March 8, 1965, the Grand Jury of Leslie County returned the following indictments against the following persons for the crimes specified:

Indictment #3122
MURDER

Indictment #3123
BANDING AND CONFEDERATING RESULTI[NG] IN DEATH 437.120

JIM HAMILTON	JIM HAMILTON
STEVE JONES	STEVE JONES
SIM GAYHART JR.	SIM GAYHART JR.
BOYD MAGGARD	BOYD MAGGARD
WORLEY ROBBINS	WORLEY ROBBINS
BOYD COUCH	BOYD COUCH
JIMMY SUTTLES	JIMMY SUTTLEY
DENNY VERNON PRATT	DENNY VERNON PRATT
BOONE BOWLING	BOONE BOWLING
WILLIE COUCH	WILLIE COUCH
HENRY P. GROSS	HENRY P. GROSS
LOUIS SHEPHERD	LOUIS SHEPHERD
FRAUD CAUDILL	FRAUD CAUDILL
LEE "BOY" SEXTON	LEE "BOY" SEXTON
	BILL PERKINS

Bond for JIM HAMILTON, STEVE JONES and SIM GAYHART JR., was set at $20,000.00 Each. All others was set at $10,000.00 Each.

Indictment #3124

JIM HAMILTON charging Assault and Battery on LESTER BURNS, Comm. Atty. Bond $2,000.00

All have been released on bond pending trial which is set for Wednesday March 17, 1965 in Leslie Circuit Court, except for LOUIS SHEPHERD who is confined in the Appalachian Regional Hospital.

DISPOSITION OF CASE: C A S E   PENDING

March 11, 1965 — Date   Report Reviewed by   Det. E. E. Wilcox / U179
Officer Making Report

XX

INV. 41
REV. 1-11-57

KENTUCKY STATE POLICE
RECORD OF SEIZED OR
RECOVERED PROPERTY

SEIZED __Yes__

RECOVERED _____

DELIVERED BY _____

FROM WHOM __Sim Gayheart, Jr. Leatherwood, Ky.__

CASE NO. __13-4924__

DATE __3-3-19 65__

POST NO. __13__

Taken from truck when Gayheart was arrested.

Item No.	No. of Items	Description	Serial No.	Value
1	1	22 cal. Colt target pistol Woodsman model	165081-S	$65.00
2	1	Leather holster	None	2.00
3	4	00 Buck 12 ga. shells	None	.35
4	11	22 cal. cartridges	None	.50
5	1	Fabric pouch with assorted bolts, nuts, etc.		.50
				$ 68.35

THE ABOVE LISTED ARTICLE RECEIVED AND CHECKED AS LISTED.

Signed _____
Responsible Officer

Date __3-9-65__

THIS IS TO CERTIFY THAT ON THIS DATE I HAVE RECEIVED FROM THE KENTUCKY S
THE LISTED PROPERTY AND HEREBY RELEASE THEM FROM ALL RESPONSIBILITY C
THIS PROPERTY.

Signed _____
Address
in full _____

' FORM KSP-2

SUPPLEMENTARY REPORT
KENTUCKY STATE POLICE

Case No. 13-4924

Radio No. ____ ____

Name of Complainant   COMM ATTY. BURNS, LESTER

Nature Request or Complaint   WILLFUL MURDER

Officers Report:

INVESTIGATION CONTINUED:

On March 12, 1965, the writer and Trooper HOMER HOWARD contacted TED LEWIS a WM 33 of Yancey, Kentucky. We were accompanied by Capt. OAKLEY WATKINS and 1st Sgt. GURNEY LUTTRELL of KSP Harlan.

TED LEWIS stated to us that he traded a British .303 Rifl to SIM GAYHART JR., about 6 months ago for other property valued at about $30.00.

He stated that at that time, GAYHARD owned several guns.

DISPOSITION OF CASE:

INVESTIGATION CONTINUED

March 13, 1965
Date

Report Reviewed by

Det. E. E. Wilcox   U179
Officer Making Report

FORM KSP-2

SUPPLEMENTARY REPORT
KENTUCKY STATE POLICE

Case No. 13-4924

Radio No. ___ _____

Name of Complainant COMM ATTY., BURNS, LESTER   Nature Request or Complaint WILLFUL MURDER

Officers Report:

On Wednesday March 17, 1965, this case was called for trial in Leslie Circuit Court by the Honorable WILLIAM DIXON. The defense, on the grounds of insufficient time to prepare their case, ask for and got a continuance to July 5, 1965.

CASE PENDING

March 17, 1965
Date

Report Reviewed by

Det. E. E. Wilcox   U179
Officer Making Report

File With Case 13-4924

L&P.

MEMORANDUM

REF. FILE NO._____

DATE __March 18, 1965__

TO: Field Commander

FROM: Commander Troop E

SUBJECT: Incident Report

On March 4, 1965 at approximately 1:30 AM to 2:AM we were in Leslie County Court House reference Case 13-4924 while Mr. Lester Burns, Commonwealth Attorney Leslie County, was questioning Mr. Jim Hamilton reference the murder of Ernest Creech. Mr. Burns first advised Mr. Hamilton of his legal rights and afterward was questioning Mr. Hamilton.

Mr. Burns asked Mr. Hamilton, "Did you see who shot and killed Ernest Creech? " Hamilton answered "No". Mr. Burns then asked Hamilton "Did you kill Creech"? Hamilton replied "No, but I'll kill you", raising to his feet and striking Mr. Burns about the face and body. At this point both Mr. Hamilton and Mr. Burns were exchanging blows and I grabbed Mr. Hamilton by the shoulders and Sgt. Mitchell grabbed Commonwealth Attorney Mr. Burns and while seperating the two, blows were being exchanged by both Burns and Hamilton.

After separating the two I asked Mr. Hamilton to sit down which he did. Mr. Burns then started questioning Hamilton reference the threat he had just made. Mr. Hamilton replied "I didn't mean it". Mr. Hamilton answered several questions for Mr. Burns and was taken down stairs to the jail.

Mr. Burns received injuries about the face and head. Mr. Hamilton received injuries, one knot on right side of right eye. If Mr. Hamilton received any more injuries they were not visable. I was advised by Sgt. Mitchell later that Mr. Hamilton's eye turned black.

Lt. Billie Lykins,
Commander Troop E

cc: File

Reviewed
3/22/65

SUPPLEMENTARY REPORT
KENTUCKY STATE POLICE

Case No. 13-4924

Radio No. _____

_M. M._

Name of Complainant   COMM. ATTY. LESTER BURNS

Nature Request or Complaint   WILFULL MURDER

Officers Report:

DATE: Wednesday March 3, 1965

ACCUSED: GAYHART, SIM JR.

A motion was made by the defense for separate trials for the defendants in this case and was accepted by the Commonwealth Attorney.

On July 5, 6 and 7, 1965, SIM GAYHART JR. was tried for Wilful Murder in Leslie County Circuit Court, the Hon. WILLIAM DIXON presiding.

After deliberating about ten minutes, the Jury returned a verdict of not guilty.

Trial dates for the other defendants in this case have not been set.

DISPOSITION OF CASE: P E N D I N G

July 8, 1965
Date

Report Reviewed by

Detective Everett E. Wilcox 17
Officer Making Report

FORM KSP-2

SUPPLEMENTARY REPORT
KENTUCKY STATE POLICE

Case No. __13-4924__

Radio No. _____

Name of Complainant _____ BURNS, LESTER _____	Nature Request or Complaint ___ WILFUL MURDER ___

Officers Report:

DATE: March 3, 1965

DISPOSITION: As of 6-11-70 there has been no additional leads in this case and no trial date has been set in the Leslie County Circuit Court.

CASE PENDING.

6-11-70		135
Date	**Report Reviewed by**	**Officer Making Report**

FORM KSP 2
REV. 5-1-71

SUPPLEMENTARY REPORT
KENTUCKY STATE POLICE

Case No. ___13-4924___

Radio No. _____

Name of Complainant __COMMONWEALTH ATTORNEY BURNS, LESTER__   Nature Request or Complaint ___WILLFUL MURDER___

OTHER AGENCY INVOLVED		Carried For UCR	
		Other	KSP
			X

List other agency involved - Determine if other agency will carry offense and arrest for Uniform Crime Reporting purposes and check proper block.

OFFICERS REPORT:

DATE: 3-3-65

DISPOSITION OF
CASE: Re: CREECH, ERNEST (Victim)

Due to lapse of time, I do not anticipate any further action on this case.

CASE INACTIVE.

9-23-74   Capt. J. A. Gay   30

Miner Fatally Shot Crossing Picket Line

Courier-Journal East Kentucky Bureau

Hazard, Ky.—A coal miner was shot to death late yesterday as he drove across a picket line at the Leatherwood No. 1 mine of the Blue Diamond Coal Co.

State police reported that the shot was fired from the midst of a group of pickets whose identity has not been fully established.

Some of the pickets have been identified with the recurring roving-pickets movement. Others are known to be members of the United Mine Workers who formerly worked at the mine.

From Perry County

Lt. Bill Lykins, district commander of the State Police, said in Pikeville the victim was Ernest Creech of Bonnyville, Perry County.

Two passengers riding with Mr. Creech said gun barrels were sticking out of all vehicles parked by the pickets," Lykins said.

"We had an earlier report that a rock thrown at Mr. Creech's pickup truck shattered the rear window as he came to work Wednesday morning. The shot that killed him was fired through the same window. Just the one shot was fired, but it penetrated his heart."

Creech, he said, was the

Col. 1, back page, this section

Miner Shot Crossing Picket Line

Continued from First Page

father of nine children. His passengers were identified as Carl Boggs, Wooton, Leslie County, and Bentley Boggs, of Smilax, Leslie County.

Reopened Non-Union

The Leatherwood mine has been the object of picketing for several weeks, since shortly after it closed as a unionized mine and then reopened nonunion.

Pickets on the line told The Courier-Journal recently that they wanted only to get their old jobs back. They charged that the company had brought in recruits from out of Perry County and out of the state when it became a non-union operation.

About 50 to 60 pickets have taken their stations from day to day at the entrance to the mine property.

State police identified some of them as being among a group numbering up to about 250 who picketed two non-union mines in Letcher County starting Feb. 16.

The Letcher County picketing was ended last week by a court order against Berman Gibson and others. Gibson was a leader of the roving picket movement of 1962, when dynamiting and shooting stirred up a round of violence. Gibson has disowned responsibility for the new roving picket movement.

DEDICATION

Lyndon Johnson's speech, given on the campus of Michigan University lauded a Great Society with abundance and liberty for all, which demanded the end of poverty and racial injustice, but most of all a society which would provide a safe harbor for the working men and women of America. In Hazard, Kentucky that speech meant little to the coal miner's struggle to survive; it would mean even less to the family of Ernest Creech.

At 1622 hours on Wednesday, March3, 1965, Earl Forest, supt. Leatherwood # 1 Mine in Leatherwood, Kentucky called and reported that an employee had been shot and killed. Detective J.E. Combs and E.E. Wilcox along with the Leslie county coroner, Dwayne Walker arrived on the scene at 1800 hours. The victim, Ernest Creech, apparently had not been moved. He had been sitting under the steering wheel of a 1950 International pickup truck; his head slumped over on the right side. He was dressed in coveralls which was soaked with blood.

His death stopped the strike, putting the pickets back to work. But for Ernest Creech's widow, Gladys, and her ten children life would never be the same. This is the tragic story of the days and months following his murder at the hands of the distraught men standing in that picket line.

This is a true story as remembered by myself, Loretta Creech, and my oldest sisters, Annette Creech Franck, Connie Creech Fowler, Dianna Creech Combs, Oneda Creech Kraner and my aunt, Earnie Carol Neace. These are the memories of the hardships and family life we knew as daughters of a coal miner in the sixties. This story is about the days following his murder and how it changed our lives. He had spent many years deep down in those mines digging and bringing coal out the hills, coal that built America as we know it today. Our father, Ernest Gordon Creech, lost his life for his family and for what he believed in. The Coal mining days, as we knew them, has now become a lost trade in this 21st century, lost to time and politics, but not to the people of eastern Kentucky. These people still cling to their traditions of the mountains and the life they knew working in the mines. I have written this book as a dedication to my family and to all the families who remembers that life in the hills of Appalachia.

This book is dedicated to my daddy, Ernest Gordon Creech. My sisters and I are thankful for having had him for the short years to teach us good values and the importance of a hard day's work. For my mommy, who had a strength through those hard years before and after his death that still amazes me to this day. I wish everyone could be blessed with the wonderful mommy we had. Unfortunately, she went home to be with the Lord in sept. of 2011 at the age of 83. We buried her beside daddy in riverside Cemetery. I would also like to especially dedicate this book to my sister Dianna who passed away in December of 2016 of pancreatic cancer. She was a beautiful woman and loved her family very much, the first of the 10 children to pass into history and we miss her very much. This book is also for my baby brother Ernest Jr. who never knew his daddy because he was born 16 days after daddy's death, and for my sisters and brothers:

Charlene, Debra, Larry and Terry who never really knew their daddy. His murder left them to be raised without a father. Also, for my sisters Annette, Connie, Dianna and Oneda, who bore the hardship of his death along and with me. They have shared their memories of their life with daddy to help me write this book. By writing this I hope my sons, Morrison and Douglas Owens, and my nephew and nieces can get a glimpse into the short life and personality of their grandfather, Ernest Gordon Creech. A lot of the memories from myself came from my diaries written while I was a student at Alice Lloyd College in Pippa Passes Ky. I had started a dairy to help me remember the life I knew with my daddy and the memories of the days following his death. I knew after I met Robert Kennedy in 1968 at Alice Lloyd that I needed to write these things down after talking to him in the cabin I was assigned to clean for his arrival. He asks me where I was from and who was my parents. I told him about the death of my daddy, and he patted me on the head and said how sorry he was, and I could almost see tears in his eyes as he spoke. I always believed he was a very kind man who really cared about me.

ACKNOWLEDGMENTS

I would like to thank my friends, Meredith Owens, the grandmother of my children from their father's side, who has now passed into history, and my long-time friends Rita Johnson and David Barnes who had encouraged me to write my story.

I would also like to acknowledge Mr. Ted Humes for the article he wrote in 1965 about the death of my father. No one could describe Eastern Kentucky during those times and the tragedy of daddy's death any better than he did in his article "No Tears for Ernest Creech." Excerpts from his article appear throughout this book. This was his opinion of Eastern Kentucky at the time—

"Much has been said of the toil and despair of Appalachia; much of its backwoods character: much has been said of its pride and poverty, of its low standards of living-of the struggle and violence. Some of the things said are all too true, but many are false and distorted. The feuding days are gone, and economic conditions have changed the whole life of Appalachia. But the spirit of the mountain people lives on, a witness to the men of long past generations who struggled against many difficulties. But still found life good. These hills ageless and inscrutable, have watched generations come and go, knowing good times and bad, booms, depression, peace and war. Eastern Kentucky has seen them all; strong in adversity and humble in success, her dignity has never been in doubt. This is Appalachia land of strange contrasts—impoverishment amid full employment, affluence and despair, misery and hope-and murder."

No Tears for Ernest Creech

ERNEST CREECH MEMORIAL FUND

A trust fund, in memory of Ernest Creech, has been established by the National Independent Coal Operator's Association.

Ernest Creech was murdered while trying to get through a picket line established by members of the United Mine Workers of America. Mr. Creech left a wife and 9 children. Mrs. Creech gave birth to a baby boy 12 days after her husband laid down his life while trying to earn a living for his family.

Ernest Creech, age 39, killed near Leatherwood, Ky., on March 3, 1965

The National Independent Coal Operator's Association, on March 16, 1965, at Wise, Virginia passed the following resolution:

"Be it resolved that a committee be and hereby is appointed, composed of not less than three nor more than seven members to solicit, accept and disburse contributions given in the memory of Ernest Creech, a coal miner, who was brutally murdered while trying to work to support his wife and nine children, and whose murder led to the indictment of pickets who were indentified as members of the United Mine Workers of America. Said fund to be known as the "Ernest Creech Memorial Fund" - Keeping in mind that the disbursement of all funds hereby collected must be solely for the benefit of, and contribute to, the best interest of his widow and, or, his dependent children."

ERNEST CREECH MEMORIAL FUND

(Starts on page 3)

After passage of the resolution the following directors of The National Independent Coal Operator's Association were appointed to the Ernest Creech Memorial Fund Committee:

Herbert "Hub" Cline, Jr., Alburn Coal Co., Matewan, West Virginia is Chairman.

Thomas Ratliff, Ratliff-Elkhorn Coal Co., Pikeville, Ky.

Louis Hunter, Paragon Jewell Coal Co., Box 354, Richlands, Va.

Ben Greer, Greer-Ellison Coal Co., Norton, Virginia.

Dave Setzer, Executive Secretary of the Letcher-Knott Independent Coal Operators Association, Whitesburg, Kentucky is fund treasurer.

All contributions to the Ernest Creech Memorial Fund should be mailed to Dave Setzer, however, any of the Committeemen will be glad to accept a donation for forwarding to Mr. Setzer.

A good sum of money was pledged at the association meeting. Many operators promised to ask their employees to contribute to the Ernest Creech Memorial Fund.

Send yours today!

CHAPTER 1
Mr. Humes' Visit

In November of 1965, an article was written by Mr. Ted Humes for the "HUMAN EVENTS" magazine out of Washington D.C... It was titled "NO TEARS FOR ERNEST CREECH" With a sub heading, A forgotten man in the great society. "The 'great society' claims to be helping the people of Appalachia, but it does nothing to protect the individual working man from union violence."

In this article he wrote, "On that grey morning as Creech's pickup truck approached the entrance to Leatherwood No.1, a piece of slate thrown at his truck broke the rear window, just missing him and sending slivers of glass throughout the cab. As one raised in an atmosphere of roving pickets and minefield violence, Creech continued to work and put in a full day down in the shaft. At noontime he purchased a rifle, fearing the worst. As he left the mine site at 4 p.m. he was met by a small army of parked cars near the entrance, gun barrels sticking out of many of them. He drove on, carrying with him fellow workers Carl and Bentley Boggs until they were blocked ahead by another car. Creech got out of his truck and tried to talk his way through. Whether or not he succeeded will never be known, because the moment he returned to his truck and sat down. A 30.6 slug ripped through and pierced his heart through the left shoulder blade. Ernest Creech, 38 years old, was dead almost instantly; Gladys Creech became a widow, and nine children lost a father; three weeks later a 10th child was born, Ernest Jr."

I wondered how Mr. Humes gathered so much information from the short visit he made to our house in late May of 1965. He came walking up Crawford road, over the bridge into our yard and up the steps to our front porch just about the time my sisters and I were coming home from school. He was well shaven, dressed in a handsome black suit, with his crow black hair combed back slick and well placed. At the time we felt he was just another "city slicker" who had come to our house to get our sad story. We had seen a lot of these people since daddy's death; people from the United Mine Workers, the Southern Labor Union and strangers from newspapers. Mr. Humes sat down in one of our hard bottomed chairs on the front porch, took out his thick black book, his shiny silver pen and started writing, asking mommy questions about daddy. Mr. Humes described mommy in his article the day he came to visit.

"She was ironing on the front porch of her frame and concrete block home situated along a dry creek about five miles from Hazard. The wooden rail was large enough to hold the pile of finished ironing. At the moment, her prime concern was a leaking roof and she had been trying for two weeks to find somebody to fix it. The dampness had given her children sore throats and they had been missing school. Finally, Charlie Campbell, a retired miner, now working on a county road improvement project, came over and started nailing tar paper over the kitchen."

I was sitting on the top of the steps with my sisters, arms locked around my knees, listening to their every word. Mr. Humes listened very intensely to words that came out of Mommy's mouth. "He just lived for his family, she said, fighting to hold back the tears. The last time he went out on strike we all but starved to death—he cried and told me he could not hold up with the union unless they fed his kids. He was good to his kids and took the boys with him everywhere he went. When Ernest was not working at the mines, he would take his truck and go out hunting junk to make an extra dollar-he did a little hunting and fishing also. He had an old outboard motor, but usually rented a boat down at buckhorn dam.... he wanted nothing more than to take care of his family."

Mr. Humes asked mommy to gather all her children on the steps going up to the front porch so he could take our picture. He described the way he saw us————

"Terry is 2, blond, barefooted and towheaded; he was playing with a plastic doll on the wooden steps leading to the porch. His brother Larry is 4 and wears a faded "Flintstone" sweatshirt and was cutting an apple which he had picked up in the backyard. Ernest Jr. is two months old now; he was born 13 days after his father's death. He was sleeping serenely on his mother's bed, a beautiful bouncy lad with curly hair; soon he began to stir, and Gladys Creech put away her ironing and picked him up to nurse him. The Creech girls are all bright and alert children; their grades are uniformly good, and they are well-disciplined, the product of good parental influence."

After he took our picture, he thanked mommy, and left. As far as we were concerned that was all there was to his visit, but in early December letters and packages started coming to our house. The mail man told mommy there were too many packages for him to deliver. The next day her daddy took her to the Post office in Hazard and they came back with a car filled with packages containing clothes, shoes, and a bunch of other things. From a large feed sack mommy poured stacks of envelopes containing cards with money. Grandpa said the things had come from California and Washington D.C, and some things had even come from a movie star, Lucille Ball. She had read Mr. Hume's article he had written about us in" HUMAN EVENTS" Magazine and sent these things to help us out. I wondered about these "furriners". They knew nothing of our life. Why did they care about us? Had they ever been up here in these mountains? Did they even know where or who we were?

Creech Memorial Fund Established

"No Tears for Ernest Creech," an article by Ted Humes which appeared in the November 13 issue of Human Events, has brought numerous letters from our readers asking how they could assist Creech's widow and 10 children.

The article, it will be recalled, related the tale of the brutal shotgun murder of Creech, a 38-year-old miner, in the coal region of eastern Kentucky. Creech, disgusted with union violence, had left the United Mine Workers and had continued to work in spite of the efforts of roving goon squads to close down his employers' mine.

Since his death, the Creech family has lived on a sparse income of contributions from sympathetic citizens in the area, together with veteran's benefits.

A memorial fund has now been established by the National Independent Coal Operators Association to help the family. Human Events has agreed to accept checks made payable to "The Ernest Creech Memorial Fund" and transmit them to the NICOA. These contributions, as gifts to private individuals, are unfortunately not tax-deductible. A committee of the NICOA has been established to disburse the funds on a basis consistent with the needs of the family.

We can think of no better way to keep the meaning of Christmas and hope for the New Year alive for the Creech family than a generous response to this appeal by our readers.

Please forward checks to:

The Ernest Creech Memorial Fund

c/o Human Events, **410 First St., S.E., Washington, D.C.**

Ernest Creech Memorial Fund

Conservatives are often condemned for lacking the virtue of charity, for failing to care for the plight of the less fortunate. Yet conservatives voluntarily aid the underprivileged through many personal welfare programs which go virtually unnoticed by the press.

The December 4 issue of Human Events announced the establishment of a memorial fund for the family of Ernest Creech, a Kentucky coal miner who was brutally murdered by a labor union goon squad. The story of Ernest Creech, whose only crime had been his desire to earn an honest living, had appeared in the November 13 issue of Human Events.

Our readers responded generously to this appeal and have so far contributed over $2,500 to the Creech family. The money has been transmitted to the National Independent Coal Operators Association, which had originally established a fund to help the family.

The generosity of those people who supported the "Ernest Creech Memorial Fund" brought the meaning of Christmas and hope for the New Year to Creech's widow and 10 children. In appreciation of the kindness extended to them, the Creech family has sent the following message to our readers:

"Bonnyman, Kentucky
January 3, 1966

"Dear Human Events Readers:

"An article in Human Events about the death of our father brought response from all over the country. To these people who took the time to write to us and to help us, we wish to offer our sincere thanks.

The Creech Family"

Human Events will continue to accept checks made payable to the Ernest Creech Memorial Fund.

4

Mr. Ted Humes

Mr. Humes wrote, "Words are poor things at the best of times: to attempt to describe the murder of Ernest Creech they are wholly inadequate. For these are the woods and the meadows that he knew and the scenes that he loved so well. He was three when he came to Eastern Kentucky from Detroit. Except for service in France with the army in World War II, this was his country."

Mr. Humes had been referring to the little community on Crawford Mountain. The road, coming up Crawford Mountain from Hazard, the county seat of Perry County, went past our house. This road was surrounded on both sides by the mountains and weaved out like a spiderweb leading to Bonnyman, Blue diamond, Typo, Grapevine, and Buckhorn. There were several hollows along the way that came off these roads and went back inside the mountains. They did not have any names. We just called them hollows.

Our lives had been typical of most children growing up in and around Hazard in the sixties. Your daddy worked in the coal mines, you went to school, did your chores, and helped with your younger brothers and sisters and wondered where your next meal was coming from. We were poorer than most but, not as poor as some. There were times, in the winter, that food became scarce but in the summer the earth provided most of what we needed. Mr. Humes gave a description of what he saw at our house the day he came to visit.

"Like most of the old company homes of this region, the Creech property is somewhat barren and run-down by modern standards. There are three bedrooms, a parlor and a kitchen; the furniture is of poor quality, walls are bare, un-plastered and the light switches hang loosely from the wall. There is a noticeable lack of cupboard space and the girls' dresses hang on open racks. The Creeches managed to secure a fairly good refrigerator and range and their only other luxury item is a TV set they bought about three years ago."

I knew we were poor and thought we would probably always be poor. I dreamed of things I knew I would probably never have. They were not big dreams, just dreams of having store-bought dresses or fancy shoes. Our school dresses had been made from the feed sacks mommy and daddy had got flour and meal in. It was a course material, but the material was decorated with purple and yellow flowers. It was pretty but the material was rough against our bare skin. Mommy was good with her old pedal sewing machine, but I still wished I could have store bought clothes. I tried to act proud of my princess style dresses, as mommy called them. Shoes were sometimes scarce; mostly we did not wear them in the summer.

Proof of Military Service

CHAPTER 2
Back to School

Mommy had sent my sisters and me back to school in late March. I did not look forward to going back to school. All my friends had given me sympathetic looks and avoided me like I had the plague. We had to mourn daddy and still try to be normal at school but there were days I just didn't want to go. Mommy was now getting donations of people from the coal company. She took us four oldest girls to the Watson Store in Hazard to buy some store-bought dresses. At least mommy was finally showing signs of life and that made me feel better. She seemed happy to be helping us pick out our new clothes.

Daddy always wanted his children to go to school and now that he was gone, I knew I had to finish. If it had been up to me, I would have quit when I reached the age to do so like some of the children around Crawford had. My grades were not good because I never liked going to school. All through my six years at Bonnyman I had to be forced to go. I threw temper-tantrums, but it never did me any good. Mommy just did not have any sympathy for me. She would drag me out of my warm bed, swipe a cold, wet rag across my sleepy face, and roughly shove my feed sack dress over my head, telling me I was going to school whether I liked it or not.

I remember my first day and how scary it was. Mommy walked my sister and me to the entrance of Bonnyman School and left us standing in front of those huge doors. To a young girl it had to be the scarest place, looking like a monster, ready to devour me at any God-given moment. I stared into the blackness of its big double doors every morning, telling myself, "I got to go in, I can't go back home." I slowly steeped my shaky legs up the concrete steps, through the doors and into its noisy, oil-soaked hall. All around me were crying, scared little faces with hands clinging to their Mommy's dress tails. I was so scared myself that I had to hold back my pee, knowing, at any moment, it was going to run down my legs. The room was musky and cold with the long dirty windows at the back of the room letting in rays of dust filled morning sunshine. Most of the children sitting around me in the wooden seats lived up the hollows down in Bonnyman, Crawford and Typo. Some were ragged, dirty and smelled. Some of them you could have probably grown a garden in their ears.

School had been useless and boring to me from that very first year. We started the day with the pledge of allegiance to the flag, right hand over heart, and the Lord's Prayer. We would then sing a couple of songs such as "Jesus loves me" or "found a peanut" before the crippled teacher, Mrs. Sizemore, would go around the room and pass out a reader to each of us. On the cover was a picture of a yellow-haired girl and brown headed boy, holding an umbrella jumping merrily over puddles of rainwater coming down in large tear-shaped drops. The book was called "Alice and Jerry", she said. We had that same book for four years. Every morning we said the pledge of allegiance, the Lord's prayer and sang those two songs. I sat at the back of the room and day-dreamed of what I wanted to be doing like playing in the creek or going upon the hillside.

I had been walking to school alone most of my first year at bonnyman because Annette, my oldest sister, had gotten sick with rheumatic fever and had to stay home in bed. I had my first encounter with death that year. It happened on one of those foggy mornings, with the dew still heavy on the grass. I noticed a pool of dark stuff in the road. The weather was warm that day, so I was barefoot, splashing my feet in the cool water in the ditch at the side of the road. A portion of the thick black substance broke loose from the poodle into the water as my feet came down. The pool had been formed from a stream running from an old toilet, which had once belonged to a burned down house. I edged my way through the weeds and briars to the door of the toilet. My feet came down right into another pool of the nasty stuff. It squished through my toes. The smell of rotting manure filled my nose as I leaned against the door to peak through the cracks. I jumped back because my mind could not believe what my eyes saw. I stood there for a few moments staring at the door, wondering if I should run home and tell mommy and daddy, or go to school and tell my teacher. I pulled at the splintered door, held by only one rusting hinge, until finally I managed to pull the door partly open. I got closer to take another trembling peek, muscles tense and ready for instant retreat. Lying there, with his bloody eyeballs protruding out onto his forehead, was a dead man. I dashed through the briars, tearing up my legs, and ran to school to tell my teacher. She gave me a strange stare and said for me to take my seat. I wondered if she believed me as I watched her leave the room and go toward the principal's office.

That evening, as I walked home from school, gloomy and sad over matters I did not quite understand, I noticed the ground where the dark stuff had been covered over with fresh dirt, and the door of the toilet was nailed up with new boards. When I got home that evening, I asked mommy and daddy if they knew about the dead man in the toilet and daddy said, "I heard it was some retarded boy from up in Blue Diamond. There ain't no telling who killed that poor boy and left him in that toilet." Well at least he's out of his misery and in God's hands now.

That night it rained and rained like all hell had burst loose. The wind moaned and the tree branches slapped against the roof of our house. Booming thunder bursts came one after the other and streaks of lightening lighted my bedroom windowpanes to reveal pearls of raindrops wavering down. I thought God was angry because someone had killed one of his children, as grandma said retarded people were. When I finally dozed off to sleep, I had a terrible dream. In my dream I saw an ugly scar-faced man coming up out of our toilet hole beating on the boy, except the boy had my face. I was afraid to use the toilet holes after that and would always look down the holes for the scar-faced man before I sat down.

We got a new principal at Bonnyman during my sixth year and things started to change. His first day he walked around the room with his back bent over our seats staring at each of us in the face. He would walk around the halls and school yard in his oversized suit trying to catch us children doing something we were not supposed to be doing. The boys stayed upon the hill beside the toilets to chew their tobacco and use their profanity. They knew Mr. McDowell would not come up there, in his nice suit, and I am sure he did not like the smell of those toilets. When the air was dead the smell from those toilets would take a person's breath. I wondered how those boys stood it up there, but I figured it was better to stand the smell then it was to get a beating with Mr. McDowell's two-by-four paddle because he really socked it hard to the boys.

Every Friday he would gather all of us in one room to listen to the preacher who came once a week to instruct us in the ways of the Bible: the "Good Book" he called it. The preacher would stand at the front of the room smiling that "I've got you now" smile, wearing his odd-colored tie so tight the wrinkles of his neck hung over the collar of his white, un-pressed shirt. He walked back and forth in front of the blackboard carrying his Bible in his right hand, telling us about the good works of Jesus and how we need to be good so we can go to Heaven to be with him. If we did not, he said, we would be going to that awful place of fire and brimstone where sinners went. Most of the children and my sisters listened with so much attention that their eyes bugged out of their heads. My best friend, Phyllis Skidmore, and I sat at the back of the room and threw paper wads. I knew I did not have to worry about going to hell because I was only ten years old. According to grandma, you were not accountable for your sins until you got to the age of thirteen. Once the sermon was over, everyone got to stay and say Bible verses if they wanted to. Annette learned all of hers and got to go to Camp National one year but not me. It was enough that I had to go to school and study I was not about to spend my free time memorizing Bible verses.

He also liked to have local talent come to school. My uncle, Jennis, mommy's baby brother, came once a week to sing and play the two cords he knew on his guitar. Mr. McDowell always let us in free because he was our uncle. I would save my three-cent milk break money to go to some special things. Once I saved my money to go to a new thing a strange man had brought to the school, a movie on a white sheet over the blackboard. I had never seen a movie before, and it seemed exciting. I walked into the dark, scary room filled with quiet children, the quietest I had ever known them to be at one of these gatherings. The movie stared Doris Day. She was a little farm girl in pigtails who sang most of what she said. I thought this was the silliest way of saying anything. It only kept my attention because it was a love story. She fell in love with this city slicker. They were talking this love stuff, kissing each other on the mouth, when suddenly the screen went out and the lights came on. Everyone got so mad, everyone except Maud, the principal's daughter. She said her daddy had turned it off because the thing was dirty. Maud and I got into a fight, and I got a wiping with Mr. McDowell's bat-and-ball paddle. Daddy and mommy said I deserved the whipping and Mr. McDowell was right to turn it off.

Most days we walked home from Bonnyman to eat our lunch. Mommy would fix fried apple pies or soup beans and corn bread. On several days, during my sixth years at Bonnyman, we went across the road to Milam's store where daddy would be sitting. He would buy us a piece of pickle bologna and crackers. Those were the days I really enjoyed spending time with daddy. He would put us on his knee and show us off to his friends and everyone would tell him what pretty girls he had. Farmer Crawford had called me "little blue eyes."

I spent most of my six years at Bonnyman sitting at my desk daydreaming, waiting for the bell. By this time, I had learned the Pledge of Allegiance to the flag, the Lord's Prayer and the two songs.

CHAPTER 3
My Seventh and Eighth Grades

I went on to Blue Diamond for my 7th and 8th grades. The bus picked us up at Melvin's store at 7:00 in the morning and if we were not right there at the bus stop, he left us. I missed it several times because I would not get out of bed. Daddy gave mommy orders that we were to get out of that bed and go every morning. I got several whippings with the mining belt over missing that bus. I still did not like school any better.

Blue Diamond was different from Bonnyman in a lot of ways. First, it had an inside bathroom deep down in the basement, but I was not about to use it because it was supposed to be haunted. A girl was supposed to have hung herself from the ceiling of the bathroom over some boy. The place was dark, damp and spooky so I believed the tale. I could not make myself pee sitting on those commodes. I felt more comfortable using the old toilets behind the schoolhouse even if they were falling in. The door would not shut all the way and the floorboards were rotted and falling in. I also had to take a chance the boys would look in on me through the cracks.

Another thing Blue Diamond had that Bonnyman did not was a cafeteria. We had walked home for lunch when we were at Bonnyman but we lived to far from home to walk from Blue

Diamond. Mommy usually did not have the quarter it cost for us to eat in the cafeteria, so she packed our lunch. It was usually a boiled egg or a fried apple pie.

Blue Diamond Coal Temple

I would smell that good aroma of the cafeteria as I sneaked up Sapphire Hallow to eat my lunch from my brown paper bag. My day was so much better when Mommy had the quarter to give Annette and me. They served vegetable soup, graham crackers and peanut butter or brownies and grilled cheese and lots of other things I never got at home.

About three months after I started Bluediamond Mr. Napier, the Principal, asked Annette if she wanted to work in the cafeteria for her lunch. Naturally, she said yes. Mommy made Annette ask him if I could work in the cafeteria too to pay for my lunch too, but Mr. Napier said my grades were not good enough to take the time out of class. Daddy thought that was great that Annette was working for her meal and I knew he wished I could too. I saw that look of disappointment in his eyes when mommy told him why I could not work in the cafeteria. I decided I had to start making better grades after that.

I did not really think school mattered that much because some of the children I went to school with at Bonnyman never learned to read and write but they were passed on to Blue Diamond with me. Some could not even spell their names. One of these children was a girl named Brenda Combs. She had belonged to a family who lived way back a hollow in Typo. I wondered if she even knew her name. Why did they even let her come to school? She stared into space with an empty stare like she was not even in this world. Her mouth stayed wide open all the time and slobber ran down on the front of her dress. She had a sister in every grade behind her, just as I did, and they all looked the same; white frizzy hair, skin so pale that they looked like they had no blood, and that awful stare and open mouth that would make a body sick. The boys at school made fun of Brenda and her sisters. They called them albinos, what that was, I did not really know at the time. I felt sorry for Brenda and had often tried to talk to her, but she would just laugh and look at me in a strange way, opening her mouth even wider. I said something to mommy and daddy one evening about the children making fun of Brenda and her sisters and daddy said, "Them youngans can't help what their folks have done, and I'd better not ever hear of you making fun of em". I did not understand what he meant when he said, "what their folks have done". I ask him but he did not answer me so after he left the kitchen, I ask mommy. She said," them youngans are inbred. Those children look that way because God has put a punishment on their folks." I still did not know what mommy was talking about, but I knew they were a strange family. Then one day while Grandma Neace was visiting, I got the nerve to ask her about Brenda and her sisters. Grandma said, "That family is a shame to God and mankind. All of them youngans belong to Roberta and her daddy and when the first youngan, Brenda, came along it shocked Roberta's mommy so much that she had a stroke and become paralyzed. She could not move anything, but her head and it was left up to old Hughie and Roberta to feed and take care of her. One summer they let her manure on herself and the fly blows got on her and killed her and Old Hughie and Roberta just buried her and went right on having babies. They had ten and would have had more if they hadn't got too old." I was not sure I understood what grandma was talking about, but I sure did feel sorry for those children, especially Brenda.

The Campbell boy from up the hollow on top of Crawford Mountain was always picking on Brenda and her sisters. I wondered what right he had to make fun of anyone because his family was not in much better shape. They may have had a few more marbles in their heads and did not look all white and sick but they never had anything to brag about. They did not want to learn to read and write and their parents sure did not care if they went to school. I believe they came to school because they liked to make trouble. They got more whippings than anyone. Mommy said their folks only sent them to school because the truant officer would get them if they did not. I totally disliked those children until one day when Mommy made me go up to their house to trade a can of commodity peanut butter for a couple of boxes of powdered milk. They lived in an area on top of Crawford Mountain where there was nothing but trees, squirrels, birds, snakes and kudzu vines. Their house was small and shabby. They had eight children and they all lived in this two-room shack that should have been torn down years ago because it was not fit for the dogs to live in. Rags and coffee sacks covered the broken windows. I had heard they half froze to death in the winter. Their folks were drunks, people said, and they stayed looped most of the time. They would trade or sell whatever they could to buy liquor. Their daddy worked odd jobs up in Hazard but every penny he made was spent on liquor. The children lived on government commodities, mommy said. She figured they would be glad to get that can of peanut butter.

As I came up to the narrow lane going to the house one of the smaller children was playing in a dirt pile. She looked up at me with her dirty, peaked face and smiled. I said to her, "where's ye Mommy?" She quickly got up and ran into the house. I followed. As I entered the door the smell of body order and liquor hit me in the face. The floors were rotted revealing the dirt underneath. Through the open windows came swarms of flies landing on the woman lying on the bed. The dresser next to the bed had no legs and three or four drawers were missing. The woman was lying with her arms up over her eyes to protect them from the sunlight streaming through the rags covering the window next to her bed. "Who is it", she said, without even looking up. "I'm one of Gladys's girls," I said, "She wants to know if you wanta trade this can of peanut butter for some boxes of powdered milk." "How many boxes does she want for that can of peanut butter," she said. "Two," I replied. "Go get her two boxes of powdered milk outa the kitchen, Geraldine," she said to her oldest daughter. When Geraldine returned from the next room, she had two boxes of milk. She handed them to me. I noticed one of the boxes had a small hole poked in the side and the powder was spilling out. Mommy had told me before I left, "be sure and get boxes that ain't been got in because them youngans are nasty," she said. The hole looked like a place where a small finger had gone through to gain entrance to food and I was not about to say anything to the woman, afraid someone would get a whipping. Anyway, I was glad to be able to give these children something to eat. They had been staring up at me with their hungry little faces ever since they had heard that I had peanut butter in my hands. Geraldine took the can out of my hand and went toward the next room. As I walked out the door, I heard the woman say to her children, "You'all go back outside and play, and you'd better not get into that can of peanut butter."

I went home and told mommy what I had heard and seen, and she said, "Them youngans won't get a bite of that peanut butter cause that old mommy of theirs, or that sorry daddy, will take it to Hazard and sell it so they can buy liquor." I wondered how those children ever got anything to eat. They always looked so hungry, and they were so skinny the wind could have blown them away. After that day I wished I could help them but after all, there were days when I had gone hungry myself.

CHAPTER 4
My Friend Agnes

D addy was out of work most of the time during my first two years I spent at Bluediamond. It was then that it really began to bother me that some of the children had nicer clothes then I did. In grade school we had gone to school barefoot, and it had never bothered me but now that I was in the upper grades, I had rather miss school then go barefoot. Mommy tried to make me, but I refused. One time, when my shoes fell apart, I took the day and walked into Bonnyman to see if my Aunt Ernie Carol had any shoes, she did not want. The only thing she had was a pair of house shoes that almost looked like a real pair of shoes, so I took them. I had a crush on a boy named Ronnie. I did not want him to think that my shoes were house shoes, but he never acted like he noticed them until this girl, who had a crush on him also, ask me right in front of him if those were house shoes that I had on. My heart sank to my stomach, but I acted proud and said, "They sure ain't, Linda Lou." My friend Agnes said Linda Lou was just trying to make me look bad to get Ronnie for herself, which worked, because she did.

It was from Agnes that I learned about the birds and bees. All through my six years at Bonnyman I thought that if a boy kissed me,

I would have a baby. Patty, my friend up the hollow by our house, said that was what caused babies to come, and she knew everything about grown-ups. Once when a boy named David Ballard grabbed me and kissed me in the school yard, I thought for sure that I would have a baby. He was dirty, his hair was very greasy, and he smelled bad. Everyone made fun of me calling me "Mrs. Ballard Biscuit." I was not about to claim him as my boyfriend even if he had kissed me. I waited and waited for something to happen, but it never did so I figured I was just lucky. I tried to stay away from him after that, but he followed me around in the school yard until I yelled at him, telling him to leave me alone.

About a month after I started to Blue Diamond I found out where babies really did come from. I told my friend, Agnes, and she told me what was going on. Boy, was I shocked! For days after that I had this weird feeling in the pit of my stomach. I told mommy about my sickness and she acted like she did not hear me. Daddy heard me tell mommy and he told her "Glad take care of that." Mommy gave me some old rags to use and kept me out of school for a few days.

Agnes became my best friend after that. I thought she knew everything. To me She was the most perfect person in the world. She was smart and had a wonderful talent, drawing. She could draw pictures of people and things that looked very real. She said her older sister, Joan, could draw even better than her and wanted to show me. She wanted me to come up to her house on Crawford Mountain to see Joan's drawings. I asked Mommy several times if I could go to her house, but she always said I had too much work to do at home. Then one day I asked her, and she said yes. I did not know why but I was so happy that I just took off with Agnes.

We walked up Crawford Mountain into an area I never knew existed. That awful snake-filled kudzu vine twisted and reached around trees, weeds ditches and electric poles. Several scaly snake skins lay upon the hot, tar-paved road flat as a pancake where the cars had run over and over them. They had probably crawled out of the thicket of kudzu, I thought. The road lay into the mountainside at an angle, making it difficult to hold yourself to the road. There was no path. You had to either walk in the kudzu or the ditch on the other side of the road up against the mountain. Either way, you were taking a chance of getting snake bit.

Mommy had once told us about a woman who had walked those curves up Crawford Mountain and had just disappeared. They found her body a week later with copperheads crawling all over her. I had thought about her tale as I climbed that road with Agnes, afraid to walk in the kudzu, the ditch or the many curves in the middle of the road, not knowing if a car was waiting around the next bend. Agnes and I climbed up that hill and went off into a narrow path leading back into the woods. It was a world of green on every side of me and the sky seemed to be barely visible. Horizontal rays of sunshine made bars in the trees as they shone down into the damp, dark forest. The smell of molded leaves along the path filled my nose. The chipping of the birds echoed in the huge woods. We followed the path for about half a mile until we came to a sunny clearing. There, alone and shabby amongst the vast forest, stood Agnes's house. It was an old camp house standing on heavy logs up off the ground. As we climbed the wooden, broken down steps leading to the porch I saw her younger brothers and sisters under the steps playing in the dirt, staring up at us, making tongues. Agnes yelled at them, "You' all quit acting silly." Her mommy and sister Joan were sitting on the porch peeling potatoes over a pan of water. "Agnes, what are you doing bringing youngans home without telling me first," she said. She did not even care if I heard her. I was so embarrassed. Agnes stopped and flopped down on the porch, acting like she did not even hear her mommy. I sat down next to her trying to get out of the sight of her mommy who was now glaring at me with a mean, aggravated stare. I tried not to look back at her, but I could not help myself. Her chin hung in three folds upon her neck and there were three large molds with black hairs sticking out of them. I looked her up and down and she did me too. I wondered how she walked on her feet. I had seen warts on mommy's feet, which she cut off with razor blades, but I had never seen as many warts on anyone's feet. No wonder I had never seen her out of this hollow, I thought, she probably could not walk.

Agnes told Joan I had come to see her drawings. Joan seemed excited, jumping up to show me the way to her bedroom. Right away I noticed the strange, musky smell of the house. I felt uneasy and would have left right away but Joan pulled out her drawings to show me and it almost took my breath away for, they were in color. Agnes did all her drawings in pencil and they were good but to see these scenes of the area around me in color were breathtaking, the shades of the trees and the cliffs above Crawford road smothered with that kudzu vine. We went through her entire drawings. One, a painting of her mommy sitting on the porch was just as I had seen her a few moments ago. The oversized face showed in detail the unhappiness I had seen in her folded eyes.

Night began to close in, so I told Agnes and Joan goodbye and started home. I had stayed longer than I intended to, and the hollow was almost pitching black. It was barely light enough so that I could find my way back out. I heard strange sounds in the forest and the whippoorwill hooted awfully close to me. I had heard them at home in the distant woods, but I had never heard them so close. I was so scared that I ran most of the way down the middle of that curvy road off Crawford Mountain. Joan had given me a drawing she had painted of the cliff not too far from the house and I showed it to mommy when I got home. "Yea, that's good," she said, and went on about her work. Daddy motioned for me to come over so he could look at it. He stared at it for a long time and said, "Them girls have got a good talent, even their daddy says so. It's a pity he won't let them go on to high school. I can't figure out fer the life of me why he takes them youngans out of school after the eighth grades. He's done all his girls like that." I thought about what daddy had said and I figured it was because they had to stay home to help their mommy. I told daddy this, but he just said, "It ain't fer us to say what a man is to do about his own. A man should be left to raise his youngans the way he sees fit, even if we don't thank its right." Agnes quit school that year.

I went to work in the cafeteria the second half of my seventh year at Blue Diamond. My grades still were not much better, but I think Mr. Napier knew Mommy and Daddy could not afford to give me lunch money so he felt sorry for me and let me work for my lunch. He came to the classroom to tell my teacher that I was to be excused an hour before lunch to help Mrs. Carter. I felt so incredibly special. Mrs. Carter was a very neat, well dressed lady. Every curly black lock of her short hair had been well placed. She always smelled so good and wore very red lipstick. Her clothes fit very tightly around her round body and she walked like it was difficult to take a wide step. I thought she was such a kind lady because she had given free lunches to the poor children when Mr. Napier was not looking. The rule was that you had to have your quarter or no lunch, but I think Mrs. Carter gave lunches to whoever did not have money for the day. I really think Mr. Napier knew she gave away free lunches, but he acted like he did not.

We formed a line to serve the food to the children and Mrs. Carter would stand at the head of the line to make sure everyone got a fair portion. Some of the children ate like they were starved to death. I think their treat of the day had been getting to eat in the cafeteria and I am sure that is the only reason some of the children even went to school. It had probably been the only meal they had got for the day. David Ballard and his brothers were always at the head of the line grabbing at every bit of food they could. I began to feel sorry that I had said mean things to him when he used to follow me around the school yard at Bonnyman. I even tried to be friendly to him but by now he hated me. I must have hurt his feelings bad, I thought. I remember thinking I would never treat anyone that way again.

After everyone was served, we got to go to the back of the cafeteria to eat our lunch. We got the same amount of food as everyone else but sometimes Mrs. Carter brought special things from home for "her girls" as she called us. She once brought a German chocolate cake. It was the best thing I had ever tasted in my life. I saved a piece to take home to mommy so she could make us one, but she just shrugged her shoulders and said, "that's Mrs. Carter's fancy cooking."

Annette graduated from Blue Diamond and went on to high school at M.C. Napier in Darford. It was now Connie and I at

Blue Diamond. Mr. Napier let Connie go to work in the cafeteria with me. Mrs. Carter liked this. She liked us "Creech girls", she said because we had been raised to work hard. It had been during my last year at Bluediamond, as I came down the steps of school to go to the basement to work in the cafeteria, that I heard an awful screeching of brakes causing me to look toward the road. A car had hit the big tree at the corner of the school yard. A deadly scream filled the air. It took my breath away. The next thing I knew Mr. Napier and Mrs. Carter came rushing out the door toward the wrecked car. I was right on their tail. As I got closer, I could see someone, a boy, half in the car and half out. It looked as if he had been thrown through the window. As I got even closer, I could see two more boys inside the car. One was down in the seat and he was not moving and the other one was almost up in the back window. I could hear him groan. Mrs. Carter had crawled into the car to see about them. Mr. Napier suddenly saw me and said, "Go back inside, ye ain't got no business out here." As I walked back toward the schoolhouse, I heard Mrs. Carter says "These boys in here are dead. This one didn't have a chance, that glass has cut him slap in half."

I watched out the window as the undertakers came to take the boys away. Mrs. Carter came back inside with bloody spots on her apron. She had a very odd, pale look on her face. She changed her apron and went on preparing lunch but afterwards, she began to cry so Mr. Napier sent her home. She patted me on the head as she was leaving and said, "are you all right". I said yes but I had an awful feeling in my stomach.

They had the funeral of the three boys in the small Baptist Church at the entrance of Bluediamond. Daddy and mommy went. Annette, Connie, Dianna and I went along with our friends from up the hollow. The boys had been laid out side by side. I walked by their caskets. I did not really know them very well because they were older than me, but I had seen them around Marvin's store. They played basketball with daddy behind the store. They looked as if they were asleep. "That's the way they are outa look, daddy informed me, I wish ye ought not seen that car wreck." I decided after that I would go ahead and quit school. Agnes, my best friend, had quit last year, but daddy would not hear of it. He said, "Agnes's daddy made her quit but I'm making you go, and I don't want to hear no more about it!" I started high school the year of 63.

CHAPTER 5
Building the New House

It was in this year of 63 that Daddy decided to build us a new house. The building of our new house had been his greatest accomplishment. He had built it with no prior knowledge of how to lay block or do carpentry. He taught himself through want and determination. That is the way he had been when he wanted something bad enough. All the other men in Crawford had added onto their old camp houses, but daddy had decided to build us a new house out of concrete block. Our old green camp house, as we called it because of its faded color of paint peeling green, daddy had bought for him and mommy right after coming back from his service during World War two. It had just got too small with a baby coming along every year. There had only been two bedrooms, one which was originally intended to be the living room, a kitchen only big enough to hold the stove and refrigerator, and a side porch where mommy kept her wringer washing machine. Its only heat source had been two coal burning fireplaces going back-to-back from the two bedrooms and those fireplaces did not even begin to keep that house warm. I remember watching the fire dance in the fireplace from the cold drafts of wind coming in through the cracks of the weatherboarding. Its damp, dark rooms with bleak, dirty chalk walls and soot-smoked windows had traces of many years of weather, life and death. I used to lie in bed at night with only my eyes sticking from under the pee-smelling quilts listening to the wind rattle the loose windowpanes and moan through the cracks of the weatherboarding. I wondered what gruesome things were lurking beyond those windows, and I imagined all kinds of eyes staring in at me. I heard things under my bed and lay rigid waiting for cold, clammy hands to run up under my covers. I just knew that house was full of un-rested souls that came out at night to torment me. I was glad when daddy finally tore it down. It only took him one summer to get the new house ready to live in. He worked on it with all the extra time and energy he could spare. Every evening when he got home from the mines, sometimes before he had his bath or ate his supper, he would go straight to work laying block. We would mix the cement for him. Shovel after shovel we loaded into the old red cement mixer daddy had borrowed off Carl Pelfrey. Day after day the blocks got higher and higher until it completely enclosed the old green house. Under the floor he poured concrete on the ground where nasty, stale black water had stood the year round under the camp house. Even in the hot days of summer when the creek in front of the house had dried up that water stood, with flies and mosquitoes hovering over it. On the posts holding the house up off the water were bunch after bunches of long-legged worms. They reminded me of maggots on a rotted piece of meat.

I saw their dead bodies floating around in the black water as we dipped it so daddy could pour the concrete. By the end of the summer of 63, it was built enough for us to start tearing down the old green house from inside and put-up flooring so we could live in it. The new house had a basement underneath, so the living area stood high up off the ground. It had four bedrooms, a living room with a big picture window, as daddy called it, a large kitchen with a back door looking out into the hillside at Ova Hagar's Garden. The door did not have any steps going down to the ground. In order to open that door mommy had to nail boards at the bottom so the younger children would not fall out. Ova would stand in that garden and hoe through most of the day in the summer. My sisters and I would stand in the door and laugh at her because she would bend over in that garden with no bloomers on. Mommy said she had never worn any bloomers because she was always pulling her dress out of her behind. Daddy would get so mad at her. He lost his job at the Blue Diamond Coal mines that summer of 63. There would be no more money to buy material to work on the new house for a while, mommy had said. He had not even put-up walls between the rooms yet. The only way I could tell where one room stopped and the other began was by the framing of the 2 x 4's. Mommy got some boxes from Marvin's store and tacked them on the 2 x 4 to make walls between the room. It was in November of that year of 63 that I first seen my daddy cry. I had known that something was wrong as I got on the bus that Friday of November 22. Everyone was crying, some sobbing like their heart was broken. I sat down in a seat next to Lonnie Napier, the only seat left. I looked at him and he was tear eyed too. What is wrong with everyone I asked. Don't you know, he said, President Kennedy was killed a couple of hours ago. I couldn't believe what he was saying. We sat silent in our seats as the bus twisted its way up Crawford Mountain to the bottom where we got off at Marvin's store. My sister, Annette, was crying as we walked up the road to the house and I felt like I had a lump in my throat. Daddy was working on laying blocks in the cold wind as we came into the yard. He was crying, wiping his nose and face on an old towel. He seemed to be more upset than I had ever seen him in my life. Mommy was in the kitchen cooking supper; her head was dropped. Mommy was not the type of person to cry, she mostly kept to herself. The days that followed was days of sadness. Daddy had gone to the top of the mountain to run the television wire to remove limbs so we could get a good reception on the television. We watched the president's funeral and cried some more. Everyone in Crawford was sad and upset. I watched their sad faces on the days I had gone to Marvin's grocery store to get our soup beans and Pepsi's. Those were some of the longest, saddest days for our neighbors and us.

CHAPTER 6
Freshman and Sophomore Years

I had been a typical teenager that year of 63 and 64, my mind consumed with boys. I was thinking that I was really grown up. My enjoyed being in the choir because I loved singing. I liked to listen to the radio at home and sing along with the music. My choir teacher had said I had a good voice and made me lead soprano. I was very proud of that. Daddy and Mommy had begun to be more lenient on Annette and me. We had gone to several parties during my freshman year and some football and basketball games in Hazard. Annette had joined the DECCA club and they had got her a job at the Circle-T, a diner in Airport Gardens just outside of Hazard. This was her first encounter with the world outside of Crawford. She said she spent most of her time behind the counter eating ice cream, something we did not get very often at home. The only time we got ice cream was on the fourth of July along with a piece of watermelon. One day she got a ride home with a man who was once married to our neighbor on the hill, Mrs. Fugate's daughter.

His car was a dark blue, fancy sedan. When Annette got out daddy was standing in the yard working on his truck. He looked at her for a while and said "He's a little old fer ye, ain't he. She told me how scared she had been when she saw daddy in the yard but that she only wanted a ride home and to ride in his fancy car. Most of the parties we had gone to had been at Skeet's Crawford's house, the daughter of Farmer Crawford, the son of the man the community had been named after, Elhanan Crawford. Daddy had spent a lot of time at Farmer's house but on the nights that we had gone to Skeet's parties he had come just in time to walk us home. He had been very protective and watched us all the time, especially if we were around boys. We played post office at Skeet's party, but I do not believe daddy knew that was going on unless Farmer told him. If he knew he never said anything. I believe he had wanted us to enjoy our teenage years. Once, he let us have a party in the basement of our house. We invited every one of our friends but not very many showed up. Daddy sat on the steps of the basement and watched us play limbo under the broom stick and laughed. I believe he enjoyed it more than we did. I saw and fell in love for the first time; at least that is what I thought, at one of skeet's parties. I saw this boy the moment he walked through the door. He stood against the wall supporting himself with his elbow. He had a look of "Mr. Cool" on his face as he stared out at all the girls with those deep brown eyes, his cold black hair fell on his forehead with a sly smile on his face. He quenched his right eye as the smoke from his cigarette drifted up his face. He dominated the room with his presence. I stared at him from the corner of my eye as "Lipstick on your Collar" played on the record player. Suddenly he disappeared, I heard a car roar off outside and I knew he was gone. I wanted to know who he was and where he was from. Skeets told me he was from up in Blue Diamond, drove a light blue 57 Chevy, was kin to the Combs boys, and was a senior at M.C. Napier. For months after that my days had been spent looking for him at school, trying to get him to notice me, which he never did, or waiting on the front porch hoping to see his blue Chevy go by our house. After months of fruitless effort, I decided I should give up and I had my first broken heart. I moped and moaned but my older sister Annette said I was being silly. Time passed and I got over my first heartbreak. I started my sophomore year and Brent came into my life. He was a freshman, younger than me, so I never told my sisters I had a crush on him. Every morning as I topped the steps leading to my home room, I seen Brent standing at the end of the hall, his books hanging loosely at his side. I saved every penny of my lunch money, hoping daddy and mommy would let us go to the football games because Brent played football and it was such a thrill to see him in his football uniform. The cool night air mixed with my romantic mood made a special time for me. Once I thought I saw him take off his football helmet on the sidelines and look straight at me, but it had probably been my imagination because he never noticed me at school, no matter what I did or how much I stared at him. The most thrilling part of going to the football or basketball games was getting to ride on that dark school bus to Hazard. This was an opportunity for my classmates, my sisters and I, to sit next to the boy we liked and even steal a kiss. Mommy no longer had to make me get out of bed every morning to go to school. I was now the first one out of bed so I could spend more time getting ready. I wanted to look as good as I could, but I did not have particularly good clothes, my hair was oily, and I had a bad complexion. I would get frustrated and missed the bus several times because I could not get my hair to look right or my clothes to fit. I cried over my complexion a lot and I knew it worried daddy because he would pat me on the head and tell me "thangs will be alright girl." I wanted to believe him, but things were not good at home. Daddy was struggling to make ends meet and we were going hungry more than usual. Mommy had been going to Hazard more often to get commodities and she brought them home in a taxicab after daddy went to work. Daddy, in the beginning, had fought her about getting commodities but after a while he began to say less and less. I think he had begun to realize that he was not going to make enough to be able to feed us. I had worried a lot about these things through the years but now these things did not seem to bother me as they had before. I was happy, thinking I was in love, until that evening March 3rd, 1965 when Grandma and Grandpa Neace came to the house to pay us a late evening visit.

CHAPTER 7
The Late Evening Visit

M r. Humes wrote "Coal mining was all he knew, and he had joined with and crossed many a picket line in his 20 years in the fields. That day of March 3rd, 1965, started out much like other days that he had experienced in this volatile and violent setting." Little did I know how my life, which I had known for 15 years, would change that day. My greatest fear, at that time, had been the bus ride up and down Crawford Mountain to M.C. Napier high school in Darfork. The bus swung out so close to the edge going up and down those winding roads on Crawford Mountain that I often wondered if I would make it to finish high school. I just knew that any day I would end up in that thicket of kudzu vine among the rattle snakes and copperheads over Crawford Mountain. Mr. Humes talked of the kudzu vine he observed the day he came to visit us in Crawford, he wrote, "One sees abandoned tipples choked by the vine running grotesquely up along the mountainside; telephone poles and even abandoned homes consumed by the kudzu—its primary function being to cover sloped and prevent slides." Brent had been standing at the end of the hall holding his books loosely by his side. I had lingered behind after the last bell, hoping he would notice me coming down the hall before I had to get on the bus. I was the last one on, so I had to stand in the aisle. I felt the nasty wads of bubble gum under the palms of my hands as I held to on to the seat rails to keep myself steady while the bus twisted and turned around the curves on Crawford Mountain. I waited impatiently for the bus to come to a halt at Marvin's grocery store to let us and the children, who lived up the hollow beside our house, off. I knew mommy was due to have the next baby, so I was in a hurry to get home fast to help her around the house. I ran up the road but was relieved to see her in the yard hanging out clothes. The wind caught her maternity blouse, blowing it up over her head to show her huge belly as she pinned the clothes to the line. They cracked in the cold March wind as I came into the yard. "Go get them youngans in the house and peel some taters fer supper" she yelled out at me. "Okay", I said, catching my breath. I did my evening chores, helped mommy get the frozen clothes off the line, got in some coal for the night and helped do the dishes. The dishes had been divided amounts us older girls, Annette, Connie, Dianna and me. That is the way mommy and daddy had it fixed. One had to wash the tin pie pans, which we used for plates, the three or four spoons and forks we had, another had to rinse them and sweep the kitchen floor, another had to dry them, and put them away and the last one had to clean the table and stove. It just so happened that this had been my job that evening and it was the job I had always dreaded.

When mommy made bread, she strewed the flour and meal all over the stove and it caked there. The children always managed to make a soup bean mess on the kitchen table, and it had to be wiped and rinsed several times. I finished wiping the table and gone to sit on the couch next to mommy near the picture window so I could watch for daddy's truck to pull into the yard. I had been hoping he had a surprise for us that night. Sometimes he brought us things home in his lunch bucket, things like a small store-bought pie or a candy bar. He left these things in his mining bucket on purpose so we could have them. Mommy divided it up amongst us. It had not been much, but I treasured the bit I got. I still see that tired look on his face as he got out of his truck packing his mining bucket in his hands, his shinny blue eyes lighting up like an owl from under the rings of his black face. He would pat us on the head, reach out his mining bucket to whoever grabbed it first, pull his mining cap off, give it to Annette or me, and run his hands through his dark, thick hair to get rid of the ring from his mining cap. We would pull the carbide lamp off its hook and take it to the creek bank, unscrew the cap and let the used carbide flow out into the rippling creek water. Daddy would then go to the kitchen to take his evening bath and eat his supper. Mommy would tack up an old quilt over the door to hide him as he bathed. I would hear them talking from behind the quilt. Sometimes they would talk about the grocery bill and daddy would accuse Mommy of running up the bill so much that he could not pay it and Mommy would blame it on him. Mommy would cry and daddy would go off to Marvin's store to cool off. He usually stayed until way after dark. Mommy had been sewing daddy's penny loafers. I was sitting there watching her hands push the needle through that hard leather. She had sewn them before with heavy thread, but they had not held. I heard Daddy telling her a few nights before to sew them with fishing wire this time. I was staring out the big picture window thinking that at any time daddy's old cream-colored truck would pull over the bridge into the yard. "Mommy, where's Daddy?" I asked. "Ain't he late getting home?" "He's probably working a double shift tonight and more than likely won't be home till late," she said. I waited at the window until only the road remained visible; finally deciding Mommy must be right. I grabbed an old, ragged patchwork quilt from my bed and went out on the porch to enjoy the cold stiff air of the evening. Mostly I wanted to get away from the fighting and hollowing of the younger kids inside the house so that I could daydream of Brent in silence for a while. The hoot owls started calling to one another from the mountains around the house. I had not known exactly where they were. I had seen the dark outline of the trees and I knew among them were the hoot owls; they called to each other "hoot, hoot, hoot". I pulled the quilt snugly around my shoulders to protect my body from the cold wind whistling across the porch and watched the tree branches move like ghostly hands against the evening sky. A shadowy dimness was slowly creeping over the earth and stillness of evening darkness came down about me. The hoot owls finally flew away, and all was silent save the whispering of the wind in the trees and the ripple of the water in the creek in front of the house. Time left me to my thoughts, the shape of Brent's face, and the way he moved up and down the halls at school. Connie had come out on the porch. She wanted to catch the bus to go to the ball game that night, but mommy told her she did not have the quarter to give her, but daddy may have it if he got home in time. The bus passed by our house on the way up Crawford Mountain as we sat there on the porch. Connie was upset. She slammed the door as she went back inside. I had been sitting on the porch about an hour when bright lights started pulling into the parking space up on the road in front of our house.

Grandma and Grandpa Neace

My first thought had been that daddy was coming home but then I realized it was not daddy's truck, it was Grandma and Grandpa Neace, mommy's parents. What are they doing out this time of night, I had thought, grandpa does not drive at night? That is what mommy had said anyway. I darted into the house and yelled to Mommy. "Mommy, Grandma and Grandpa is here" "What in the world are they doing out this time of evening," she said in a startled voice. They came across the bridge up the steps and through the front door. Uncle Jenise's wife Pauline, stood next to grandma with her arms folded, looking scared and upset. Grandpa had said to mommy, "Gladys, where's Ernest?" "He's probably working late; he's been doing that often." Mommy had said, "I tried to tell him not to work late this evening because he was sick with the diarrhea this morning when he left, but I guess he is working late anyway." "No," Grandpa said, "they shot him and he's dead." Mommy became dumbstruck and her mouth flew open in disbelief. She threw down Daddy's shoes and hurriedly went past me. I heard Grandma say to Grandpa, "hush Matt, you'll scare her to death." Grandpa's words had hung in the air like an echo over the mountains. I began to feel panic rising inside me. I could hear Mommy crying and screaming at the top of her lungs out on the porch. I followed her outside. She started running up Crawford Road as fast as her legs would carry her. Grandma immediately started to shout for mommy to stop but she was not listening. She disappeared out of sight over Crawford Mountain. Then I heard grandma say to grandpa, "Matt, we'd better catch her and take her to the hospital cause she's going to have that baby anytime now." Several awkward seconds of silence followed. I watched the lights of their truck fade over Crawford Mountain and then Aunt Pauline, Annette, Connie, Dianna and I gathered our younger brothers and sisters together and took them back into the house out of the cool night air.

CHAPTER 8
Daddy Comes Home

I sat on the couch through the night, staring out the picture window into the cold darkness, feeling the cool night air creep in around the cracks of the window. Daddy just could not be dead, I thought, it had to be a mistake. Why would anyone want to shoot my daddy? I just did not understand. I fell asleep several times only to be awakened as my head fell against the cold windowpane. Finally, I must have dozed off to sleep. The next thing I was aware of was the breaking of day. I raised my head and the bright glare of the morning sunlight hit me in the face. The sun was peaking over the mountains, casting a shadow over the porch. The bandy rooster crowed. I remembered him crowing two nights before as we were going to bed and daddy had said to Mommy, "Glad, that roosters got his time mixed up, ain't he?" Mommy had not said anything. She just rolled her eyes and shook her head because a rooster crowing at night, according to Grandma Neace, was a sign of death and Mommy was a firm believer in the signs.

The early morning silence ended abruptly as voices sounded loud from outside. I then noticed a bunch of our neighbors, Mrs. Combs, the Fungates, Marvin, the store owner and some of the other miners around Crawford, gathering around a large black car parked at the top of the road. The people looked strangely and sadly at one another. The two men in black baggy suits were talking to our neighbors and putting things in their hands. They came slowly across the bridge and onto the porch. The door swung open. A cold draft of wind swept through the house and froze my bare feet. Time after time the people came into the house bringing wooden folding chairs reading "MAGGARD FUNERAL HOME" on the back, two lamps with long shiny metal posts and milk glass shades and a purple velvet cloth on medal stands. They sat them at the back of the living room in a semi-circle. The room quickly filled with chairs and people, but mostly there were flowers. Bunch after bunch of flowers filled the living room as the people came, carrying both arms full. I had never seen so many flowers. They had a cold smell of death about them like the flowers I had seen on the graves in the small graveyard on top of Crawford Mountain.

The house became packed with people. They found themselves a place to sit on our old broken-down couch in the living room or in the kitchen on our lard cans. They huddled close together and whispered to each other. Some dropped their heads in silence and others stood against the wall staring out like they were waiting for something to happen.

Daddy in Casket

Uncle James, Mommy's oldest brother, had arrived and seemed to be taking charge of everything. He was the preacher in our family. I remember his becoming a preacher with his baptizing in that muddy Typo River. I was small but I still remember watching from the banks of the river as a strange man took Uncle James out to the edge of the bank and ducked him in that muddy water. Something great and holy was supposed to have taken place, according to Grandma Neace.

Uncle Jennis, mommy's youngest brother, was with Uncle James and they were talking to each other. I could not hear what they were saying but I could tell Uncle James was giving him instructions by the waving of his hands and the pointing of his fingers. Then the men in black suits said something to our neighbors and my uncles. They all went back outside to another black car which had just arrived. The two funeral directors opened the big doors behind the car and pulled out a long shiny, silver casket. It glistened in the morning sunlight. Over the bridge they brought the casket, up the steps to the porch and edged it through the doorway. They brought it over and sat it in the semi-circle of the purple velvet cloth.

My brothers and sisters were now awake and standing at the door of their bedrooms, scared eyes glaring from dirty faces of yesterday's play. They shivered in the cold, wondering who all these strange people were in their house. I was dressing my baby sister Debra when I noticed that everyone had suddenly got incredibly quiet. Uncle James very gently closed the front door and the two strange men in black suits took a place at each end of the casket, hands folded in front. Then the one on the left cast an uneasy glance to the one on the right and nodded his head in acknowledgement. The man on the right then stepped out in front of the casket and opened it up. My hands flew to my mouth and my stomach felt as if I would get sick at any time. My heart was pounding, and I could barely breathe. There before my eyes was the face of daddy. He is dead, I thought. Tears flooded down my cheeks as I walked closer to the casket. My older sisters were crying, sobbing like their hearts were broken. Daddy looked so peaceful lying there in his light blue shirt and matching dark suit jacket. I had never seen him so dressed up except the time he had gone to Ohio to look for work in the factories. I walked over and touched his cold hands. One looked larger than the other. I could see that the wrinkles of his hands were still filled with coal dust. I had heard him complaining to mommy on several evenings that he just could not get all that old coal dust off his hands.

Crying was coming from behind me out on the porch. I was glad mommy was home. The thought had crossed my mind that she might have that baby and die but she had not had the baby yet. Her maternity dress was dirty, and her curly black hair stuck out around what had once been a ponytail. Her face looked pale and sunken against her high cheekbones. Mommy's screaming and crying became louder the closer she got to daddy's casket. Finally, she collapsed and fell to the floor. Grandma and the funeral directors ran over and grabbed her, taking her by the arms to lift her into a chair. One of the funeral directors held something white to mommy's nose and she threw up her head like she had been shot. Her tear-filled eyes flickered like a bright light had been shining in them. She got back up again and started leaning over the casket holding daddy's hands and rubbing his face. The funeral directors and Grandma pulled her away and sat her back down in front of the casket. She sat there; her sun-browned hands lying on her lap, whimpering. Finally, she relapsed into silence.

CHAPTER 9
The House Fills with Mourners

The morning progressed as I sat in those cold wooden funeral chairs. There seemed to be more and more people showing up. The breeze of the cold evening air came in the room in every direction as the front door opened repeatedly. They brought more flowers and put them around the casket. It was surrounded by attentive neighbors, women whispering to each other, their faces saddened as they looked at daddy in his casket and over at my brothers and sisters and me. People came from out of the hollows, people I only saw on Election Day. They were leaning up against the wall, silent with their thoughts. Some moved about the house noiselessly with drawn faces.

Agnes, my friend from school, had been standing close to the door with her sisters, brothers and her mommy and daddy. This had been the first time I had seen Agnes since she had quit school during our first year at Blue diamond. Her mommy stood close to Agnes. She had on a pair of shoes cut out for her many corns.

The noise increased around the room with the arrival of more and more people. Many of the voices were familiar to me. Standing not too far from the door were the Campbell's. I thought about that can of peanut butter mommy had sent with me that day to trade for some powered milk. I often wondered if those children got any of that peanut butter. The children had always been ragged and dirty at school and they were still dirty as they stood over in the corner staring at me. I had heard daddy talking to mommy about the Campbell children a couple of weeks before he was killed. He said, "Glad, I seen one of them Campbell youngans down at the store this evening and he was begging fer food. I bet them youngans ain't had nothin to eat for a long time. Why don't their folks feed them and keep them clean, Glad. Anybody can afford a bar of soap and a pan of water if they wanta!"

People were crying leaning over mommy to whisper their regrets, saying "Gladys is there anything I can do to help?" Mommy never answered them. She just kept her stare at daddy's body. Around the room came unending low voices, whispering to each other. I was listening to every word. I heard Farmer Crawford say to his wife, Marg, "What's poor Gladys going to do with all them mouths to feed and poor Ernest dead?" There was a slight crack in his voice as he talked. I looked up at him and gave him a curiosity stare because I had been thinking the same thing myself.

Farmer touched me lightly on the shoulder as he passed through the room. I had never seen Farmer in anything except a pair of bibbed overalls and his baseball cap, which he never took off except to scratch his head. I had thought how odd that cap looked with the suit he had on today. Farmer's wife Marg was crying. She was taking her apron to wipe her eyes and nose. Skeets stood close to her mommy trying to give her comfort. Her long silky blond hair covered the top of her dress. She had always worn such nice clothes and smelled of soap and perfume. Elhanan was staring at Daddy's face in the casket. He was struggling against crying, but a few tears slid down his cheeks. I walked up to him and he patted me on the head like he often did the homeless dogs around Crawford. Maybe he is thinking about dying himself, I had thought. He was old but his mind was sharp. I had stood at the top of the road many an evening just to watch him pass as he walked up and down the roads of Crawford. It gave me a warm feeling when he smiled at me.

Grandma Neace stopped to talk to Farmer and his family for a moment. She was telling Marg that mommy had tried to walk all the way to the hospital down Crawford Mountain to see daddy's body, but they had finally got her in their car. She said the nurses tried to stop mommy from going into the morgue where daddy's body had been laid out on the table, but mommy fought them and went in anyway. This made me feel sick inside.

I followed grandma as she went back into the kitchen. She was trying to figure out how to work the big coffee pot the funeral directors had brought. I reached out and stuffed a piece of chocolate cake into my mouth as I talked, "Grandma", I said, "There sure is some strange people around here. Do you know any of em?" Words failed her as she dabbed at her eyes. "Yea", she said, "I know that fellow over there in the plaid suit" She pointed to him. "That's Luke Combs. He owns that liquor store in Blue Diamond. You've probably heard ye daddy and mommy talking about him. I know ye had to pass that liquor store every morning as ye went to school at Bluediamond." I knew who she was talking about and I did hear Mommy telling daddy once about some girl that had killed herself on the hill above the liquor store over one of Luke's boys. She had taken some poison and was begging for him to take her to the doctor to save her life, but she died right there on the hill anyway. Died in his arms, mommy had said.

Uncle Jennis's wife, Pauline, was trying to help in the kitchen. She opened the oven door and took out a plate of food that mommy had put there for daddy's supper the night before. She started to throw it away, but my sister Connie grabbed it and said, "Don't throw that away, that's daddy's supper." Pauline put the plate down on the table and started crying as hard as she could. Grandma reached over to comfort her. I tugged at Grandma's dress, trying to get her attention because I wanted to ask her about these strange people in our house that I did not know. "Do you know that man standing by the door? He has been here all morning long and was here last night", I asked she was wiping her nose on her apron as she answered, "Yea", she said, "that's Willie Dawhare. He owns that clothing store in Hazard where I buy ye aunts' clothes." I did not know where that store was because I had never been there. I had only gone to Hazard a few times in my life when mommy took us there to get shoes or see Santa clause. Most of the time she just measured our feet with crochet thread and went to Hazard to buy them herself. I did know about the nice clothes my aunts, Alice and Ernie, always wore. I had wished I could wear clothes like that from those fancy stores in Hazard, but we never had the money like Grandma and Grandpa did.

CHAPTER 10
Grandpa Creech and Grandma Dona Visit Their Son for the Last Time

From the kitchen I could see a man ducking his head as he came through the front door. It was Grandpa Creech. He started shaking hands with everyone in the room. I motioned for Grandma Neace to look. "Well, I swear", she said, It's ye grandpa Creech." This had been the third time I had seen Grandpa Creech in my entire life and that had been a few years back. I had not recognized him at first. The first time I saw him I was only eight years old, and we still lived in the old camp house. He had come in a taxicab a few days before Christmas. Daddy had been at work. Grandpa had been drunk so mommy put him in a bed next to the Christmas tree in front of the window. There he lay drunk as a skunk, still clutching his liquor bottle, his long legs sprawled out on the bed when daddy came home from the mines. Daddy undressed him down to his boxer shorts and forcefully took his liquor bottle away. Grandpa took a fit. He cursed at daddy and tried to sling his drunken arms to hit him. Then he tried to get up and feel backwards into our Christmas tree. The thrones of the pines stuck into his butt and he yelled bloody murder. He cursed and fought the tree and we laughed so hard our bellies hurt. It was a sight to see, his big, long hairy legs sticking up out of that decorated tree. Grandpa finally passed out for the night and we had our usual Christmas. Santa visited by our beds to leave our toys after we had gone to sleep and the next morning, we got up to play with them. Grandpa got up sober and helped us play with our new toy top. He sat in the middle of the floor and played with that top in between those long boney legs and acted like a child. I really did enjoy his visit.

Daddy and Grandpa Creech

The next time he came to visit was noticeably short. A taxicab pulled in front of the house. We had all been working in the garden. Grandpa Creech got out, so drunk he could barely walk. This made Daddy mad, and he started yelling at him. Grandpa got back into another cab and left. Daddy was terribly upset for days after that and he threw a temper tantrum on mommy and they got into a big fight. I knew he was being mean with mommy because he had been upset with his own daddy.

Daddy's parents had divorced when he was three years old, and grandma had remarried. Mommy said grandma divorced Grandpa Creech because he drank too much and beat on her. I always figured that that was the reason daddy hated for anyone to drink and he would not touch Liquor. Mommy said daddy had got drunk once with his mining buddies on moonshine up at the coal mines, but he had got so sick he almost died. He had not touched it since.

Grandpa Creech was moving around the room talking to everyone like he had known them all his life. He was drunk, as usual. Farmer and some of the other men in Crawford were trying to get him to sit down and be quiet but he just got louder. He had gone over to the casket to stare at daddy's body. He turned around to mommy and said, "Gladys I told Ernest not to go back in them mines years back. Now ye see it's got him killed." Mommy never answered him. She dropped her head to avoid looking at him. Finally, some of the men took him outside. Grandma Neace told Aunt Pauline that they'd better get him out of there before Bill, Grandma Dona's husband showed up.

Grandma Dona and Bill

It was not more than an hour before the door opened and Grandma Dona and Bill came through the door. Grandma Dona was crying as she made her way toward her son's casket. Mommy looked up, her lips were trembling, and she began to cry again. Grandma Dona passed out and fell to the floor. Bill tried to catch her, but her weight was too much for him. They both went to the floor. Grandma Neace came out of the kitchen to help. They finally got Grandma Dona up and sat her down beside mommy. Tears were streaming from Bill's eyes. Grandpa Bill put his arms around grandma, and she put her face into his breast and sobbed. Grandma Dona did not even have on her make-up or earrings, things she had always worn. She had always been such a good dresser with her store bought dressed and fancy pump shoes. She looked as if someone else had dressed her that day, probably her husband, Bill. They had always been awfully close, and I never remembered them being apart.

Grandma Dona House in Hazard

Bill and Grandma Dona once owned a beer joint up in Hazard. Daddy had never approved of her running that beer joint. He would fuss every time she came to visit us which were not very often. There had been many fights at that beer joint and one killing, daddy had said. I had only been in that beer joint once. Daddy had gone to ask grandma to borrow some money. He took Annette, Connie, Dianna and me with him. The beer joint was dark and musky, smelling of liquor. The floors were oiled just like the floors in Bonnyman grade school. There was a bar in one half of the room and a wall of liquor on the other side. I thought it was the most exciting place in the world. Daddy sat behind the bar and talked to his mommy while we sat on the rotating bar stools and rolled around and around. Grandpa Bill had given us a whole candy bar and a pack of chewing gum and we were really enjoying ourselves. I wanted to go back and visit them again, but daddy said it was no place for children. They had sold the beer joint years back and moved to a farm in Laurel County.

Daddy's Sister Audrey

I wondered why daddy's sister, Audrey, had not showed up since daddy's death. She was the only sister daddy had and he did not have any brothers. The closest thing he had had to brothers had been Grandma Dona's brother, Donald's sons, Jimmie, Woodrow and emery. I had only met Aunt Audrey a couple of times. The time I remembered most had been the time daddy and mommy took us to London to visit Grandma Dona and Bill at their farm. Audrey and her husband, who was French-Canadian, and their three girls, Cindy, Linda and Pamela had lived in a huge white house out in the country. Daddy had taken us by their house on our way back home to Perry County. Aunt Audrey had a collection of comic books. She let Annette, Connie, Dianna, me and her three daughters go through every one of them. It had been very hot, and we sweated so much sitting out in the grass that my hands had stuck to the covers. Aunt Audrey yelled at us for tearing up her comic books. Her husband moved them to Wisconsin shortly after that and we had not seen her since. I guess she just lived too far away to make it to daddy's funeral. I knew Daddy had loved her a great deal because he talked about her all the time.

Daddy with Boyhood friends

Daddy and Audrey

Daddy at age 4

49

CHAPTER 11
The Neighbors Settle in
to Stay the Night

G randma Neace leaned over mommy and whispered, "Gladys I'm going to the kitchen to fix ye some coffee. You'll drink some fer mommy, won't you?" Mommy did not move or answer. I followed grandma into the kitchen and sat down at the table. The big coffee pot went blob, blob as it worked to make the coffee. The aroma seeped into the air and smelled good enough to eat. I remembered smelling that aroma seeping into my bedroom in the early morning hours as mommy fixed it for daddy before he went to the mines. The low, soft warmness of mommy and daddy's voices had given me a feeling of warmth and that coffee smell reminded me of that feeling.

Grandma went into the living room to take mommy a cup of coffee. Maybe I will sneak and have a cup while grandma is not looking, I thought. I knew that if she caught me, she would call me down and maybe even backhand me. I was about to put the coffee to my mouth when a voice came from behind me. "That'll stunt ye growth," Mrs. Fugate was saying to me. The deeps of her eyes looked troubled. They followed my hands as I put the cup down. She had a bowl of green beans in her hands and put them down on the table next to me. They were still steaming. Her eyes were glazed with tears and she whipped her nose on a clean white handkerchief.

A fast-moving step approached behind me from the living room and my friend Patty and her baby sister, Barbara, sat down beside me at the table, her short skirt coming up to mid-thigh. "Who are all these people?" she asked. She was all peppy; acting like this was a social event. "I don't know" I said in an aggravated manner. As usual her bleach blond hair was teased high on her head and she had on lipstick. Now why did she want to dress like she was going to a party to come to my daddy's funeral, I had thought. I got mad at her and got up to go back into the living room.

Patty's daddy was standing next to mommy's chair. He must have worked in the mines that day because there was still a ring of cold dust around his eyes. He and daddy had been good friends for many years. He spoke to grandma, "how are you 'all doing?" His hand on grandma's shoulder seemed to shake and his voice trembled. His hair, which had been white ever since I could remember even though he was the same age as daddy, had streaks of black coal dust throughout it.

Our house was now filled with more familiar faces. Lizzy, who lived up the hollow beside our house, was dragging Connie out onto the porch. I went to the window to see where they were going. They stood next to each other with their backs against the railings of the porch staring at all the people coming and going.

Lizzy had been an incredibly quiet child ever since she had been hit by the car in front of the house. She had a lot of scars on her arms and neck from the accident. We thought she would die, and she was in the hospital for a long time, but she finally got out and was all right. Daddy had felt sorry for her. I could tell by the sad way he looked at her when he called her "little squirt".

Annette's friend, Mary Ellen, was in the kitchen washing dishes with her mommy. They had always been such neat people. I was sort of embarrassed that they were washing our dishes. I knew they ate out of fancy plates and nice shiny silver forks and spoons. I wondered what they thought about our pie pans and bent forks and spoons. I knew they had come from a big city somewhere to

Crawford and did not live like most of the other people around here. Mary Ellen's mommy was genuinely nice to everyone, even though she kept mostly to herself and took care of her family. Her big sister had moved away shortly after the family moved to Crawford to work in Washington D.C., Mary Ellen had said. I had always thought how strange it was the way Mary Ellen had kissed her mommy in the mouth before she left to go anywhere with us. I never remembered mommy ever kissing us.

Mr. and Mrs. White, Mary Ellen's neighbor in the hollow, had come into the house carrying two pies. Tears had begun to come to Mrs. White's eyes as she walked closer to Daddy's casket. I had never known kinder faces then those of Mr. and Mrs. White. Daddy had depended on them lending us hoes when we worked in the garden. They always seemed happy to lend them to us. Daddy took good care of their tools and returned them promptly. Mrs. White's floppy gray hair fell about her face as she bent over to examine daddy in his casket. Then tears came down her face in a flood and her husband came over to comfort her. His kind old face creased into sadness. I remembered mommy once saying he had a real bad problem with his heart and should not get upset.

Uncle Donald and Bertha

Aunt Bertha, daddy's uncle's Donald's wife, was now taking care of the food in the kitchen that people had brought. She moved around the kitchen placing a bowl here and a bowl there. She had always been like that, wanting things to be proper and perfect. She looked thin, and her dress hung almost to the floor as she looked up at me over her glasses. We had visited her house often through the years. Her long, huge wooden table always had a pouring jar of kayo syrup sitting right in the middle all neat and well placed. Mommy didn't like to go to her house, and she wouldn't eat there at all because Bertha had bunches of cats running around her house. She would tell daddy that cats belonged outside, not in the house.

Uncle Donald had been at the house ever since they had brought daddy's body home. I had watched him pace back and forth from the living room to the kitchen. He had gone by daddy's casket several times to stand and stare at daddy's body. Daddy and his uncle Donald had looked a lot alike, everyone had always said that, and they had been awfully close. He had his head dropped most of the time except to talk to his wife or one of his sons. Daddy had been awfully close with his cousins, Woody, Emery, and Jimmie and the one daughter Miranda. He had spent a lot of time at his uncle's house on top of Crawford Mountain. The cousins would walk by daddy's casket and stare at daddy for a while, walk away then walk back up to it again.

Mrs. Fugate and Mrs., Stevens from up Crawford hollow, had come in through the door with their passel of children clinging to their long dresses. Mrs. Steven's youngest child was hanging onto her long black hair which hung down to the back of her legs. The child had reminded me of another child she had had, the child that had been run over by a cold truck on her way home from school one evening.

I had already reached home when I heard her brothers coming up the road crying, telling mommy their little sister, Judy, had been run over by a coal truck. The truck had flattened her and there had been no hope for her. The people who lived around Marvin's store had spread a blanket over her body and waited for the undertaker to come to get her. They had sent all the other children home, including her brothers.

This child had often come to our house to play. I remembered her angel-looking face and long silky blond hair. She was always hungry. She would beg mommy for food. Mommy would get mad but would always give it to her, saying "that old mommy of hers is more interested in her holy-roller religion then she is in her youngans." Daddy had told mommy that anytime that child came to our house hungry she was to feed her, no matter if we had to divide what we had. For a long time, she was at our house every day. I thought of that child's hungry looking face staring up at mommy as I watched Mrs. Stevens move through the room that day.

The other lady was Mrs. Fugate's daughter-in-law. She handed me a big bowl of potato salad. I took the bowl to the kitchen and put it in the middle of the many other bowls of potatoes salad. The sour smell of mustard seeped up my nose and made my mouth water. A part of me wanted to just sit down and start eating some of everything on the table. This had probably been the most food there had ever been on this table, I thought. There was every kind of food a body could want. Hunger had gnawed at the pit of my stomach for the last several hours, but I could not put the food in my mouth. The bit of cake I had eaten earlier had sort of made me sick.

I went back into the living room to check on mommy. "Mommy, are you all, right?" "How's the youngans?" she said. "Go keep an eye on them and make sure they're fed and warm." I went back into the kitchen where my younger brothers and sisters were humped up against the wall with their chins against their chests. I suddenly realized night was upon us and the day had gone. Annette, Connie, Dianna and I picked up our younger brothers and sisters one at a time and carried them off to bed. Mommy gave a nod of approval as we went past her. I knew all these people in our house were planning to stay up all night with daddy's body and I wanted to stay up too but I had grown so tired that my mind had become blurred with sleep, so I crawled off to bed.

CHAPTER 12
Getting Ready for the Funeral

I woke up early the next morning. The bright glare of morning sunlight streamed through my bedroom window. It looked like such a glowing morning that I had almost forgotten about the awful news of the day before. Then I remembered everything and popped up in bed. I quickly rolled out and wrapped my still warm quilt around me. A cold damp air had filled the house. All was quiet except for the clearing of throats here and there. People were sitting around the living room in funeral chairs, humped up under their coats and blankets, some asleep, some half-asleep. Mommy was still sitting in that same chair, wide awake. She looked exhausted and spirit-less. "Mommy," I said, "are you all right?" "You'd better go put some coal in the stove fer ye brothers and sisters get up." she said. Her voice was weak and small in the silence.

I shivered from the cold as I made my way down the shaky wooden steps leading from the kitchen to the basement. The cold wind whistled through the cracks of the small soot-smoked window next to the stove. Through the spots of clear windowpane, the sun was trying to come through. The big mouth of the stove was still a little warm, so I knew there must be some red cinders. I opened the door and shoved a big block of coal into its mouth. It caught fire, crackled, and a large blaze shot up. I shook the bottom of the stove for the ashes to fall through.

Topping the stairs from the basement to the kitchen I saw grandma moving ghostlike through the dim kitchen light. She was putting water into the big coffee pot. Turning around to me she spoke quietly. "There's a woman here who's going to get you youngans dressed fer the funeral. Go get ye brothers and sisters up." Her voice came across as tired and irritable. Annette, Connie, Dianna and I had to practically pull our younger brothers and sisters out of bed. They were crying and fighting to stay in their warm beds.

I put on my coat and went outside to see what the weather was like. The day, which had looked so warm out the windows, was now blowing a cold wind-driven snow. My body became chilled, and my hands and feet ached from the cold wind slapping me in the face. Water ran from my eyes and nose. This seemed to be the coldest day I had ever known in my life.

As I came back into the house, this woman dressing my younger brothers and sisters, handed me a warm washrag to wash my hands and face with. I did not know this woman very well, but I did remember being at her house once around Christmas time. Her family had invited my sisters and I and our friends in for a cup of hot chocolate one Christmas evening. We had been sleigh riding up the hollow beside their house behind Marvin's grocery store. Her family must have had money because she and her brother dressed nice, and their house was fancy and proper. I remembered how the rugs on the floor sank as I walked into the room and the silky white curtains on the windows moved like a leaf falling to the ground as the wind swept into the room. I believed they had been deeply religious because there was a Bible on the table next to the door and paintings of Jesus on the white walls. Beautiful Christmas decorations were all around the room with a huge Christmas tree in the middle lighting up the entire room with bright colored lights. She had led us into their kitchen, giving us fancy decorated Christmas cups to drink our chocolate from. The warm steam had felt so good against my face that cold Christmas evening. We sang Christmas carols with her family and then went home.

She seemed to be overly concerned with us today as she washed the dirt from my younger brothers and sisters faces. She gave my older sisters and I some store-bought clothes to put on to wear to the funeral. They smelled new. I wondered where they come from, so I asked the lady. She said they came from Willie Dawahare's store in Hazard. He had given them to us, she said. I felt so proud of my brown jumper with the long-sleeved blouse underneath and the long tie hanging down the front.

Last picture with Daddy

Grandma was in mommy's bedroom trying to get her to lift her arms so she could put a new maternity blouse over her head. Her arms dangled weakly. She was too tired and weak to know what was happening. Grandma saw me and said," gather ye brothers and sisters together and take them outside and get into the big black car at the top of the road." She drew a long breath and sighed uneasily. Annette, Connie, Dianna and I took our younger brothers and sisters outside into the snow filled wind to put them into the huge black car. There were cars lined all the way down to Marvin's store and people were getting into them out of the snow. Grandma Neace and the funeral director brought mommy out and put her into one of the long black cars. She was still crying. Out the window I watched the snow come down hard on the funeral directors' black suits and daddy' silver casket as the funeral directors and mommies' brothers carried it down the steps of the house he had built, and across the bridge he had built, and slid him into the back of the hearse. One of the funeral directors came to the car we were in and brushed the snow off his suit before getting into the car to drive. I pushed my nose against the car window as it moved up and down Crawford Mountain, the wiper blades swishing back and forth to move the snow aside. The car came to the bottom of Crawford Mountain and turned to go to airport gardens where my uncle's church was, the "Church of the Lord Jesus Christ". The cars climbed the muddy hill up to the church.

CHAPTER 13
The Funeral and Burial

The man driving got out and told us to wait in the car. Grandma Neace finally came over and told us to get out and go into the church. Ernest Maggard, the funeral director, was now standing at the church door shaking hands with people as they came through. He was pointing at places inside the church for them to go. His nature was stern, dealing with the sad, grieving people. Each person stopped for a moment at the door to sign their names to the wine-colored book on a stand before going in. He pointed to the front of the church to a place we were to sit behind Grandma and Grandpa Feltner.

After all the chairs were filled, people started lining themselves around the room, leaning against the wall, hands folded in front. The people from the United Mine Workers and Southern Labor Union stood close to the door. "Ernest was awful young to die" I heard Aunt Bertha say as I sat down. "It's a shame he had to die that way and leave all these youngans behind. I heard he was shot with a high-powered rifle, right through the truck, and bled to death in just a few minutes," she said to a strange woman sitting beside her. My stomach turned upside down and my hands shook. Uncontrollable tears flooded down my face as I listened to her talk.

Suddenly I felt trembling hands upon my shoulders. I looked up into my Great Aunt Dellie's face. She eased into the seat beside me, tossing my sister Debra into her lap. Alice, mommy's younger sister, sat down on the other side of me and took my hand, patting it for a few moments. She was very frail. She had rheumatic fever when she was incredibly young, and it had left her with a bad heart. She had been sick most of her life. She was only 25 but the doctors had told Grandma Neace that she would not live much longer if she did not take care of herself. Aunt Earnie Carol, Mommy's baby sister scooted in next to me and took Larry into her lap. Grandma had let Mommy name Ernie Carol after daddy. She had married daddy before Ernie was born. She was only a few years older than Annette and me.

After everyone was in that wanted in, Mr. Maggard closed the door very gently and took a seat beside Mommy and grandma Neace in the front row. An odd silence fell over the room as Uncle James stepped up to the casket, loudly clearing his throat. He shook his head mournfully and placed his right hand on top of the casket and began to preach in a low, slow, mournful tone. "Ernest has gone from this earth. We should not mourn for him because he has gone to a better place. A place where there is no suffering." He then quoted verses from the Bible, verses saying that daddy was not dead, that he was only sleeping until God came back to earth at the end of time when he would take him to Heaven to be with him. As he got more and more into the sermon his voice got louder and louder, drawing breaths between sentences in loud gasps like each breath was his last, yelling praise the Lord after each sentence. Amens were coming up from all parts of the room.

I wondered what Daddy would have thought about having this Holy-roller sermon for his funeral. He had never really said much against the holy rollers, but I somehow believed he did not exactly approve of them from some of the things he had said. He had often laughed when Irvin, our neighbor on the hill, complained about the holy rollers making too much noise on the hill at Tarie's store. I remembered what he had said when we slipped off and went up there to watch the holy-rollers dance and carry on. Their preacher, brother Abe, was a noticeably short man in a large suit who could give the most soul raising sermons anyone could want to hear. He would have the people up dancing all over each other and shouting their words in tongues and it was a treat for us to see. We thought it was the most exciting thing around Crawford. When daddy found out we were going up to the tarie's church just to make fun of the holy rollers he warned us that we had better not go up there again if we were going to make fun of them folks. "I know they're silly", he said. "But ye ain't got no right making fun of people's religion."

When Irvin had died and they had a holy-roller sermon for him, at the request of Mrs. Fugate. Daddy had said, "Boy, if old Irvin knowed that brother Abe was preaching over him, he'd probably get up out of the casket and curse him out". Mommy had said, "Well, it won't help none because if anyone's soul is hell-bound its fer sure old Ervin." Daddy laughed and said, "Now Glad, if anyone can force Irvin's soul into heaven it's that brother Abe."

James's sermon that day had been just like Brother Abe's. His booming voice battered into my ears. Everyone was screaming and crying and some even getting the Holy-Ghost and speaking in tongues. Finally, after an hour of this commotion, Uncle James's voice got softer, and the people calmed down. Then he raised his hands and started with a song, "Precious memories, how they linger, how they ever flood my soul." Mournfully, all the people took it up and sang it like it came straight from the depth of their souls.

Mommy had often sung this song the same way as she sat on the porch in the dusk of the evening rocking the babies to sleep. Daddy would stand at the edge of the porch staring out into the mountains, the light of his cigarette glowing in short puffs in the darkness. The mountains would slowly fade into darkness as mommy's voice whined, the whippoorwills making their lonely hoots, and the crickets making their never-ending noise in the stillness of the night.

Another hymn rose, a slow mournful song, "Everybody I met seemed to be a rank stranger", and "I'll fly away, oh Glory, I'll fly away. When I die hallelujah by and by, I'll fly away," The music was loud and full of emotion. There was a lot of handclapping and "hallelujahs" and "praise the Lord". It brought tears to my already washed-out eyes. Finally, he stopped the singing with a wave of his hands, and everyone lowered their heads for prayer. It was a heart-dissolving prayer, full of sorrow sobs. "God bless our family and deliver us from these suffering, Lord. Be merciful upon this soul of my brother Ernest Creech and take him to Heaven on that great judgment day to be with you forever in that great place where we may see him again, dear Lord, and have mercy on our souls, Amen.

After the prayer, the crying came to a stop and there was silence except for the clearing of throats and blowing of noses. Mr. Maggard then took the floor and said, "Thank you Brother Neace for that wonderful sermon." Then he motioned for the people at the back of the room to come forward. The sound of chairs being pushed back filled the room as people made their way in sympathetic silence to view the body. Some of the people went by slowly, shaking their heads as if to say, "what a shame." Others, like our classmates from up the hollow, went by the casket as fast as they could so they would not have to look. We were last. As I rose from my seat a sick feeling came to my stomach, a feeling that traveled up into my throat like something had lodged there. My hands were shaking as I hurriedly moved through the rows of chairs, fearing my courage would fail me if I delayed. I knew this would be the last time I would look upon my Daddy's face. My sisters were crying like their hearts were broken and they probably were. We were still sort of in disbelief that this just could be true, that he was dead. I threw my baby brother terry up on my hip and quickly darted outside with the rest of the people. It was now snowing so hard you could barely see the outline of the mountains. The day was now the color of ash. It was as if the sun had ducked out of sight forever, leaving the world cold and white. I could hear mommy's cries coming from inside the Church. The casket had been closed and the funeral directors were rolling the casket toward the church door. Grandma Dona was trying to get them to open the casket back up so she could get one last look at her son, so the funeral director opened it up one more time for her. She's trying to pick Ernest up out of the casket," I heard Ursula Eversole say. I turned around and crossed my arms and dropped my head because I did not want to see this. Grandma Neace and the funeral director came out of the church dragging mommy across the mud-covered road like she could not walk. They put her into the car behind the hearse that had carried daddy's body. Grandma hurriedly said to me as she passed, "Get ye brothers and sisters together and get back in the car ye come in".

The big snowflakes were pounding hard into my face, laying upon my eyelashes. I could hear the crinkle of the leaves as the snowflakes fell into the bare trees in the woods surrounding the church. I lead my brothers and sisters to the car. Out the window I watched the big snowflakes accumulate on Mr. Maggard's crow black hair and bushy eyebrows. He lined the cars in rows behind us. His nose was red from the cold and he moved stiffly. I could hear his voice rumble like distant thunder as he gave orders to the cars to line up in rows, dusting the snow from the collar of his coat before hopping into the front car with daddy's casket. We were on our way, where too I did not really know. The car was cozy and warm, the seats as soft as Mrs. Fugate's feather beds. I pushed my nose against the car window watching the snow make a world of white over the mountains. The car turned into Riverside Cemetery, the cemetery right outside of Hazard just a few minutes up the road from M.C. Napier high school. I wondered why they were burying daddy in this fancy cemetery. This is the place where they burry rich people, I thought. Everyone else in Crawford, who had died, was buried in the cemetery on Crawford mountain. I had been up there venturing through the woods. It was almost always covered out of sight with year after year of autumn leaves. I wanted daddy to be buried there too so I could visit his grave when I wanted too. How I was going to get over here at Riverside Cemetery, I thought.

My feet sank into the snow-covered mud as I stepped out of the car. I tossed my baby brother Terry up on my hip again and headed toward the spot with my sisters where everyone was standing. The snow filled wind swept into my face and against the aged marble stones as I made my way around the sunken graves. Chairs from the funeral home had been placed around a hole which, I knew, was to receive daddy's body. In the chairs sat Mommy, my Grandmas and

Grandpas and mommy's sisters, Alice and Ernie Carol. Uncle James said a few more words over the casket. His voice echoed in the wind. The words were short and quickly said, because he too was probably about to freeze to death. He spoke of daddy going to Heaven to be with God. I hoped he was right. I wanted to think that despite his swearing and cursing, God would take into consideration that he was a good man in his heart and take him to Heaven. The thought had crossed my mind, several times since I had realized that he was dead, that he might go to that awful place of fire and Brimstone where sinners went, according to brother Abe and Grandma Neace.

The shiny silver casket sat at the edge of the hole with snowflakes pounding hard against its top as Uncle James finished his short sermon. Aunt Alice had gathered us together to lead us from the graveyard. I turned to look over my shoulder as I walked away. They were lowering the casket into the ground. I will never see daddy again, I thought, at least not in this lifetime as Uncle James had said.

Riverside Cemetery

CHAPTER 14
Life after Daddy

Girls and Friends

The months of April and May of 1965 passed slowly. The earth woke to life again and the mountains turned to green, purple, and yellow. Spring had usually brought a new world to me, the birds tweeting and moving in the trees and that fresh smell of blooming flowers, but to me the world had still been cold as if winter were here to stay. A gloom hung over our house and a sickened, lost feeling filled the pit of my stomach. Crying seemed so useless to me. My sisters seemed to be lost and sat on the porch most of the day with their friends staring out at the road like they were waiting for something or someone. We had been so used to having chores do every evening, now we had nothing to do after school but watch our younger brothers and sisters and help mommy with the cooking and washing. Most days we counted cars going up and down the road. We each picked a color of car to see who could get the most of their color at the end of the evening. I liked to pick blue because that was daddy's favorite color. We knew daddy was not going to be pulling into the yard every evening to see if we had done our chores and mommy did not care anymore. He had been so strict about cleanliness. He made us sweep and clean the basement every other day and the coal dust from that concrete floor was always so nasty.

My sisters and I would choke, and daddy would tell us to put a little water on the floor to keep the dust down. He made us mop the floor in the living room and kitchen almost every day and the torn piece of rug had been extremely hard to mop. We did not dare to sit down until everything had been done. Sometimes it was late into the night before we finally got to sit down to do our homework before going to bed. I used to dread Wednesdays because that was the day daddy had designated mommy to do the washing. In the summer she had done the washing on the front porch. The wringer washing machine had to be filled over and over to wash and rinse. It had not been too bad on those warm days but when the days got cold mommy had washed in the kitchen. The water of the dirty laundry ended up on the kitchen floor. We had to mop and mop to get it all up and then the nasty water had to be emptied out of the washing machine through the back door and all the clothes hung out on the line in that cold air. Our hands would freeze to the point of bleeding from being chapped. They had stayed that way through the winter. Most of the time mommy would hang them out herself because she did not want us out in the cold even though she was usually pregnant. After he died mommy would wash clothes only when we needed them, and she only did one load at a time. It did not take up the whole day. We played in the creek and did much of nothing. There had been many donations of food from everywhere after daddy's death. We had been given so many loaves of bread that we had to get Mrs. Fugate to put some in her refrigerator. The United Mine workers had given mommy money to help, but just until mommy could start drawing checks from the government, they said. London Clemons, from up in Bluediamond, had told Marvin to let mommy have anything she wanted at the store and to charge it to him. Mommy did because the food people had brought during the wake had started to run out. That is the way we had survived for the month of March and some of April. People from around Crawford and in Hazard had done everything they could to help but I knew this would come to an end. I wondered what we would do if the state did not help us. I felt responsible because I had been the second oldest, especially since mommy seemed to have lost interest in almost everything. I worried and wondered if we would survive without daddy. In the dim grayness of those evenings, the dust of darkness just sitting upon the earth making things to look to be what they are not, and, according to Grandma Neace, ghosts make their first nightly appearance, I could almost swear, on several occasions, that I had seen daddy sitting on this porch of this house he had built with a smile on his face. I wanted to believe the smile meant he had made his peace with God before he died and had gone to Heaven where someday I would be able to see him again.

CHAPTER 15
The Last Time I Saw Daddy Alive

My life in Eastern Kentucky as a young girl had been filled with things I did not quite understand. The mountains surrounding me kept the world out and me in. There had always been tales of ghosts and things up in the mountains that kept me afraid. I had listened to the grown-ups and tried to take in as much as I could, but my parents and grandparents believed that children did not need to know details about most things, thus the big secrets about daddy's death. At the time I just knew he was dead. I did not really know why, and I never understood the true circumstances of his death. I am not sure I fully understand it now. My grandma Neace, mommy's mommy, had been filled with sayings. She always had those "off the wall" comments about things. Most of what she said I did not pay much attention too because that was just the way she was, but something she had once said kept going over and over in my mind throughout that year of 1965 and still to this day. She said, "God warns people one way or the other that their time is close at hand." I wondered if she could have been right because I remember the strange things that had happened, and the way daddy had acted the night before he had been killed. That evening, Tuesday, March 2nd,1965, had been one of those dark,

dreary overcast days. The day had drug on and on. I thought the
day would never end. It was on the hazy side of darkness as I got off
the school bus at Marvin's store and started up the road toward the
house, walking gently pulling the dripping icicles hanging off the
cliffs along the side of the road to suck on. The wind was blowing
icy cold as I darted into the house. With our evening chores done
and nothing to do in the dull twilight of that cold, dark afternoon,
mommy, my brothers, sisters and I had gone to bed early. I could
hear the wind making a moaning sound as it whipped around the
side of the house. Long into the night I lay in bed, unable to sleep,
watching daddy's shadow on the living room wall reflected by the
dim lines of light coming from the kitchen. He was sitting at the
table with his head buried in his hands. The house was quiet, and
his shadow only moved as he shifted his tiring position. Something
profoundly serious must be bothering him, I had thought. I lay
there remembering another time he had sat at that table through
the night. About five years back he had witnessed one of the boys in
Crawford, David Miller; die in a car accident up in Blue Diamond.
Daddy had come upon the accident just as it happened. I heard
him telling mommy about it as he ate his supper that evening.
"Glad," he said, "It was awful. David was caught in the door of that
car. Blood was coming outa his mouth. He gave that death gurgle,
rolled his eyes in his head and died." Daddy's voice had sounded
sad and shaky as he spoke. All kinds of thoughts kept going over
and over in my mind as I lay there in bed that night. Two nights
before, I remembered hearing mommy and daddy talking about
pickets being outside the mines when he came out to go home.
They had thrown slate at his truck window and yelled "scabbier" at
him. Some men had even been carrying guns, daddy had said. He
told mommy he intended to stop at the company store to purchase
a rifle on his way home from work the next evening. He meant to
use it if he had to, he told her.

Mommy had said to him, "Ernest, I'd rather fer us to starve then
fer you to get ye self-killed." Daddy laughed like he had been glad
she was concerned then assured her he would be all right. My sister,
Connie, next to me, tossed and turned with an occasional groan.

In the next room I could hear my sister, Dianna, made a snorting, sucking sound as she sucked her thumb in her sleep. Upon the mountains in the distance behind our house I could hear Clarence's dogs howling at the moon, making shivers run up and down my spine. I pulled my patchwork quilt up around my neck and lay stiff and silent, thinking, dogs' howling at night is a sure sign of a death in the family, according to Grandma Neace, but after all they were Clearance's dogs, not ours. Car lights, from the road in front of the house, lighted up the living room in a moments flash, leaving behind that shadowy darkness. I had been lying there for hours thinking, listening to the sounds of the night, watching daddy's shadow on the wall, until finally I could not stand it anymore. I slipped from under the warm covers, crawled overtop my sister, and tiptoed over the cold creaking floor, through the living room and into the kitchen. Daddy looked up at me as I came into the room, but never said a word. I pulled a lard bucket from the corner of the kitchen and plopped down. I wanted to ask what was bothering him, but the words just would not come out of my mouth. I knew he would probably just tell me to go back to bed and to not be sticking my nose in things that did not concern me. I propped my elbows on the cold metal table and starred up at the fly-spotted light bulb hanging by a cord in the middle of the ceiling. I wondered if he had been upset about the argument he and mommy had had earlier in the week. Mommy was complaining about our wobbly kitchen table and the electric stove, which only had one burner that still got hot. Daddy had been telling mommy he just could not afford to get another stove right now. This one, which he had got from a used furniture dealer in Hazard a couple of years back, had to do until he could afford to get another one. It looked like it would be a while before daddy could afford another stove because mommy was expecting another baby in a few weeks, which meant another mouth to feed. I was in a daze, staring at that fly-spotted light bulb, when Annette strolled into the room rubbing her sleepy eyes. Daddy looked up again, the light shining in his bright blue eyes. He glanced at her and said, "Whata ye girls doing up this time of night? Ye oughta be in bed." I was afraid to say anything and was making moves to get up to go back to bed when he spoke again, "Whata ye girls wanta do when ye get outa school?" "I wanta go to college," Annette said. "I do too", I said. He kind of laughed as a look of admiration came over his face. "Ye girls have done good in school and I know you'll make me proud."I went back to bed wondering why he had brought up a thing like school at such a strange hour of the night. He was still sitting at the kitchen table with his head in his hands as we slipped back off to bed.

CHAPTER 16
Changing times

Through the year's things had sometimes gotten hard, but daddy and mommy always managed to work together so they could provide us with enough to survive. Most of our food had come from the earth and daddy had known every way possible to make the earth provide for his children.

His pride and joy had been his beehives that he had brought from the woods one at a time and sat on the hill above our house. Twice a year, he had robbed these hives and filled jar after jar with honey and comb and mommy had stored them under the house for the winter. She had made him a helmet out of an old hat and some mess wire to protect him from the stings, but the bees never really bothered him. The hives had sat on the hill looking all broken down and deserted in the fall of 1965. Weeds had grown up around their little wooden homes. I did not hear or see them buzzing around the strawberry patch like they had done every year. It seemed as if they had known he was gone and returned to the woods from where they came. Grandma Neace had said animals and insects know things like that. I had known that the honey was something we would not be able to depend on when winter came again and probably not the strawberry jam and jelly mommy had made every year either.

Daddy's strawberry patch, sitting next to the beehives on the hill, had blooms that summer but they had not come on like they usually had. We had a few strawberries, but they were small and few. I had known it would not be long before they would die out altogether. Without daddy's special care, weeding and transplanting plants as he had done every spring, the patch would not do very well, and mommy was not going to make us weed and take care of it the way daddy had. We canned a lot of strawberries from that patch, and we picked strawberries when they were ripe until our fingers got sore. I did not believe I would miss picking those strawberries, but I knew I would miss eating them but most of all I would miss seeing daddy bent over in that strawberry patch.

The things my sisters and I had been made to do every year, from the time we were old enough, did not seem important to mommy anymore. If daddy had lived, our garden would have already been planted and the young bean sprouts would have been sticking their curled heads from under the ground. In my walks through the garden spot, I had noticed the hard mounds of dirt, long ago depleted of its minerals from year after year of planting, had been naked and cracked against the sunny sky. The Farmer's Almanac, daddy had used to plant his garden by, lain stained and ragged upon the table where mommy kept her flour and meal.

Every year daddy had tried to grow more and more in his gardens so mommy could put up enough food to last us through the winter. Five years before daddy's death Grandpa Neace had told daddy he could use his land down in Typo to plant an extra garden spot. The Typo River overflowed its banks every spring and the land was very fertile. We had grown things in this garden that we had not been able to grow in the garden behind the house, things such as watermelon and muskmelon.

When the signs were right for planting, according to the Farmer's almanac, daddy had loaded us four oldest girls in the back of his old cream-colored truck to take us to Typo. The sun would just be coming up over the mountains as we slowly moved down the gravel road through the dense blanket of morning fog. The morning glories would still be open on the sides of the road and the earth would smell of morning freshness. The movement of the truck through the cool early morning air would make my face so numb I could barely feel my cheeks. The moisture in the fogy air filled my lungs so that they almost felt like bursting. By the time we parked above the garden spot my face and clothes would be damp. I would grab my hoe and make my way through the wet morning weeds behind daddy and mommy and my three oldest sisters down the path leading to the clearing of the garden spot over the hill. The dew still clung to the leaves and beamed like sparkling diamonds in the early morning sunlight.

Everything was incredibly quiet and still throughout those days. The only sound being the constant chop, chop of our hoes. It was a lonely sound making the days pass slow and empty. Occasionally we would hear distant voices from across the river. I often wondered to whom those voices belonged. I had never one soul on the other side the whole time I had spent down there, but I knew there had been a family who lived way back up the hollow around the mountain in the woods. They were inbred, their father and granddaddy were the same person, grandma had told me, and he kept his daughter/wife locked up in the house because he did not want anyone to get near her. I heard Grandma Neace tell mommy about a dead baby found floating down the river in a shoe box. They knew it was theirs because of the way it looked.

The glaring heat of the midday sun would press down upon our heads so intensely in that garden spot that several times a day I had felt my hair to make sure it was not on fire. The coolness of the fresh-turned earth against my bare feet and an occasional stir of air had been the only relief from that blistering sun. I thanked God for each small stir of air. I lost many a drop of sweat in that rich soil, made blisters on my hands and busted them again on the hoe handle. I saw the sun go from cool in the mornings, to blistering hot during the day and back to cool again as evening closed in.

Sometimes, after we came out of the garden in the evenings, we would stop at our great uncle Hager's store. Hager was the brother of Grandpa Neace, Mommy, s daddy. Sometimes uncle Hager would give us a Pepsi and they never tasted any better than it did on those hot evenings. Daddy would point us toward the Coca-Cola cooler where Uncle Hager kept his cold drinks. He had never kept much inside his dusty store. There had always been a cardboard box of dingy, what had once been white, shoestrings sitting on the counter and a few cans of food on the shelves that had been there so long the labels were faded. There were large bags of meal and flour on the floor, which, mommy said was probably filled with weevils. He had rolls of bologna in a cooler which he made sandwiches for the people coming and going. He was friendly to us but never gave us a free bologna sandwich. Mostly he sold snacks and drinks.

Aunt Dellie, grandma's sister, lived over the hill in one of Uncle Hager's camp houses. She and her husband Charlie would be sitting on their porch over the hill or in front of the store. I had often seen her walking the roads of Crawford on her way to and from Hazard with her paper bags of used clothes she had collected there. She sold them very cheaply to people up and down the road to help those who could not afford to buy new clothes. I believed she had a heart of gold because of this. I thought she would die at any time because she was so skinny and coughed a lot. Mommy said she coughed so much because she smoked too many of them cigarettes. She always carried her pack of Camels in the pocket of her baggy sack dress and always had one lit between her fingers puffing away as she talked and done business. Daddy liked Charlie, which surprised me because Charlie was a drunk and daddy did not like drunks. Charlie had large pockets in the lining of his suit coat where he carried his half-pints. He stayed "looped" all the time, as mommy would say. He and daddy would spend hours, until way after dark, talking on the porch, daddy puffing on his cigarettes, Charlie sucking on his bottle of liquor.

Camp House in Bonnyman

In later years daddy had been working a lot at the mines so mommy and us four oldest girls had to do most of the gardening by ourselves. We had to walk that gravel road through Bonnyman into typo. Stretches along that road had no houses at all, only the mountains on both sides of that narrow dusty road. I had to move slowly over that graveled road that hurt my bare feet. We never got as much work done as we did when daddy was with us. Mommy never worked us as hard as he did. Every now and then she would say, if she thought we weren't going to get as many rows of corn or beans hoed out as we should she would say, "you' all better get them rows hoed out cause ye daddy will wope ye." When the vegetables got ripe, we had to walk that mile and half stretch back up the road with those burlap bags of ripe vegetables slung across our shoulders, and we carried them as full as we could. The juice of the tomatoes would run down the back of our legs, blistering them, and the burlap bag would cut into our skin like wires.

CHAPTER 17
No More Canning

Mommy as a young girl

Mommy had canned everything from the garden, except for what we ate during the summer. Some things could not be canned, things such as potatoes, squash, melons and onions. We kept them stored under the house for as long as they would last. We had a "tater" bin next to the steps going underneath the house and we filled it as full as we could, but they never lasted us through the winter. Green beans had been the hardest vegetables to can. The jars had to be washed very carefully or the beans would ruin. They also had to be cooked outside under an open flame in mommy's old wash tub for hours. Annette, Connie. Dianna any I had to wash, string, break up the beans, stuff them into jars and keep the younger children out of the fire and the rags snugly around the boiling jars. It was usually after dark before mommy came out of the house, with the smell of the evening meal in the air, take the jars out of the water, tighten the lids, and sit them on the porch to cool overnight. We would get water from the creek to pour on the red embers, listening to their hissing in the quietness of the night, before going to bed. The beans would sit on the porch until morning when mommy would once again tighten the lids and take them to the basement to be put on the shelf with the other jars of canned stuff put there by long days of hard work. This year of 1965 there would be no green beans to can and probably would never be again.

We also canned peaches. Daddy would buy them from a truck that came through Crawford every summer. We had a bathtub daddy had put in just a year before he was killed, and he had filled it full of peaches that year. Us girls had sit on the edge of the bathtub and pealed those peaches until our hands got raw. I grew to hate peaches and the fuzz off the skins made my skin crawl. Peaches had been daddy's favorite fruit and he made us can as many as he could afford to buy. I had spent most of my summers wishing the man with the peach truck would not show up, but he always did. I do not believe I saw the peach truck that summer of 65. It would not have mattered anyway because mommy said she could not stand to look at a peach. The basement had been completely empty of can stuff and potatoes the day daddy had been killed.

It was a slow-moving summer that year of 65. In the past our summer days had been full of working every waking hour to gather and can everything we could to last through the winter. Things like the green apples which belonged to our neighbors to the right... Their place, with its large shaded, well mowed, carpeted yard, was paradise to me. Where I went when there was not anything around to eat. Laura and Willie did not like us going into their yard without their permission, so we had to sneak over there when they were not home to get the biggest apples. Willie's mommy would watch us if she could from her yard, two houses down on our left. She would stand out in her yard and stretch her neck trying to see if we were over there, but I knew a secret way and old Ova never caught me. I would save my apples in my pocket for hard times. Old Ova and Laura liked daddy. Twice or three times a year they would give daddy permission to send us girls over to their yard with brown paper pokes to gather apples. Laura and her mommy would stare at us with a mean look, knowing we had probably just been over there last night when they were not home. We bent over gathering them as fast as we could so we could get out of there. Mommy would take the apples, cut them in quarters, stuff them in jars fill the jars with water and two aspirins, like the ones we took for headaches, and sealed them tight. They came out of the jars in the winter as crisp as the day they were put in. She also made apple butter, apple sauce, and apple jelly. The kitchen always smelled of cinnamon and spices on the day's mommy made the apple butter. The neighbor's yard had filled up with apples in the fall of 65 but I hadn't eaten even one because we had plenty of food from all the groceries mommy had gotten at the store.

Blackberries was another fruit we gathered and canned in the summer. They bloomed and became ripe every year during the month of June, and we picked as many as we could. There had been two places daddy had liked to pick blackberries. One was in a place called Sapphire Hollow. This had been his favorite place because we could get buckets of berries in no time at all. Sapphire Hollow had been a deserted mining camp up behind Bluediamond grade school. It had once been a booming coal camp, but what had once been houses were now empty, fallen-down buildings with blackberry briars and weeds in the yards where rose bushes once bloomed. The best patches had been around the opening to the mine shaft at the end of the hollow. I could feel the cold air coming out of the hole as I bent over to pick. Mommy did not like picking berries up sapphire hollow because she was afraid of snakes. I had heard rattle snakes shaking among the weeds as we picked. Daddy would wade through the weeds like snakes did not exist and he expected us to do the same. Mommy's favorite place to pick blackberries had been upon the hill across the road from our house. We would leave the house at the break of daylight so we could pick as many berries as we could before the sun got too hot to be able to stand it amongst the weeds. The heavy mist and fog would hide the path as we fought our way up the hill to the top where the sun shined, and the blackberries grew. Squirrels would drop acorns from the trees above our heads making an echoing "blob" into the large woods and the birds would sing "pretty, pretty, pretty." I would answer, "thank you, thank you, thank you". The morning air would slowly turn to a miserable heat as the sun beamed down upon our shoulders. I would come down that hillside, trying to sooth my burning legs from the briar scratches and chigger bites, looking out over the mountains at all that open space wondering if God was looking down upon me from one of those mountains. I pretended to be a bird running down the hillside letting the wind catch me and lift me off my feet. Daddy had often called me down; afraid I would stumble and fall down the mountainside. The blackberries had come and gone that year of 65. We did not pick one bucket, not even to make a cobbler.

CHAPTER 18
Killing the Hog

During my walks up the hill behind our house that summer I had noticed how the hog pen standing in the middle of the garden spot had looked so empty. This had been the first year there had not been a hog in that pen waiting for his execution when fall set in. That mound had smelled bad on those hot summer days. I had to stop up my nose to be able to pour his slop over the sides of the pen into the trough. He would snort around in it for a while before he finally ate it. We feed him scraps from the table but most of the times we did not have scraps to feed him because it was all eaten. These were times when we had to go to our neighbor's house to ask for their slop. I always hated doing this. I went to school with their children and going to their house to ask for slop was very embarrassing. I either went or got a whipping with a keen limb, something I dreaded worse than asking for the scraps.

We fattened the pig through the spring and summer and killed him in the late fall. Daddy would let us know a few days ahead of time when we needed to get things ready for the kill. Water had to be boiled in the big washtub in the front yard so the hairs could be scalded off the body and a place had to be fixed between two big trees to hang the body so it could be gutted.

Daddy shot the pig in the head with his twenty-two rifle. It would squeal as it went to the ground, wiggling and jerking. Daddy then took mommy's big butcher knife and slit its throat, steam from the blood rising in the cool autumn air. "The meat's gotta be bled to be good", mommy would say. The body was then laid on a board and we would pour boiling water over it. We had to take knifes and scrap the hair off the limber body. The skin would fold in its layers of fat as my knife scraped across its pinkish skin. The longer I scraped the colder the body and my fingers got. Its body was then hung between two trees to be gutted. My stomach always felt a little sick as I watched daddy take mommy's butcher knife and pull it through its stomach, the guts falling into the washtub below, steam and a foul order rising in the air. He would then reach into its belly and pull out the remains that had to be torn loose, blood up to his elbows.

We kept the liver and stripped the fat from the guts to render for lard, throwing or giving away the heart because "its bad luck to keep it", mommy would say. We kept the head and feet. Daddy had especially liked the head. I knew I could look forward to seeing that hog's head staring at me from a big pot on top of the stove a few days after the kill. He said I was being silly because I would not eat the head, feet and tail but I just could not put them in my mouth after seeing its head staring at me as I feed it. I sure could not eat that fatty greasy tail or the feet after watching it stomp around in their own manure. The day after the kill I would go to the empty hog pen and there would be a jelled pool of blood next to the gate. I knew there would be another poor baby pig in this pen to be raised and fattened and butchered the same way as its former occupant. That year of 65 I looked over into that pen knowing there would never be another pig inside that pen. Mommy would never butcher a hog the way daddy had. The manure and slop, which the former occupants had pushed out the sides of the pens, had hardened to crusted mound around the boards and the smell had completely gone away.

I spent most of my time that summer sitting and thinking. My favorite place was on that hill under the huge oak tree in the garden spot next to the little bee houses. There I could look out over the mountains. For the first time in my life there were no strawberries or blackberries to pick, no canning or working in the garden, no gathering apples or killing hogs and no sweeping that dusty basement floor. My time was my own, except for watching after my younger brothers and sisters. Mommy would go to the big grocery store, the J&R, located at the bottom of Crawford mountain and get groceries. She had money that came from the government and bought what we wanted to eat. She still cooked for us every day, but it was not the same. We never gathered around the table tp eat like we use too. We would each get a plate of food and go on the porch or in the living room. I did know that I did not have to worry about where our next meal was coming from, it came from the government.

CHAPTER 19
Ernest Jr. is Born

Thirteen days after daddy's death Ernest Jr. had been born. There had been seven girls, Annette, me-Loretta, Connie, Dianna, Oneda, Charlene, and Debra, born to mommy and daddy before their first boy, Larry, was born. I had fond memories of the proud smile on Daddy's face when he came home from the hospital and told us we had our first baby brother. He even went in debt again at the Kentucky Finance, borrowing money to buy our first T.V. The next year Terry, my second brother was born, and daddy beamed and bragged to all his mining buddies. I know he would have really been proud of the birth of little Ernest Jr. if he had lived to see him born. I heard Grandma Neace say, "Gladys died on that table when that baby was born but the doctors brought her back to life, I thank she wanted to die." Mr. Humes described mommy in his article the day he came to visit: "Gladys Creech is tall, with deep-set blue eyes. In spite of her solemnity and sadness, she gives the impression of a woman quite young: in spite of the tragedy there is a certain repose and serenity as she strives to preserve her calmness. She is calm but, in her breast, there is no lack of painful wounds; they would have been married 20 years this December. Mommy had cared extraordinarily little about anything when she first came home from the hospital, only taking little Ernest to feed him when he cried with hunger. She never said much, just sat around rocking back and forth in her hard-bottomed chair. Her crying had ceased and been replaced by long, lost stares. Sometimes she had sung those old religious ballads as she rocked the babies to sleep. I had fond memories remembering how her days had been filled with doing things daddy invented in his mind for her and us to do. Things like trying to can rhubarb, which she argued with daddy that rhubarb could not be canned but of course he believed it could. In the end he won out and he would grow more and more of it each year and mommy would make rhubarb pies in the winter. She was always taking time from her cooking, canning and us children to help him do something. He was thirty when she took our schoolbooks and taught him how to read and write. He had only gone to the third grade and had never learned to read and write very well. After Mommy helped him, he became enormously proud of his ability to read and write, often borrowing books from his Westerfield cousins. The last book he read was *The Last of the Mohicans.* It lay on the dresser after his death in his and mom's bedroom, faded and torn. He got his driver's license after he learned to read and write. He did not have any choice. A state Trooper had stopped him one evening as he came home from the mines and told him he had to get his driver's license if he was going to drive his truck. Mommy was up late every night for a month teaching him the driver's manual so he could take his driver's test. He failed it the first time, but they stayed up late a few more nights and the second time he passed. I know he never would have passed that test if mommy had not helped him. She had always loved telling us the cute little story of how she and daddy met. A bright twinkle would come into her eyes as she told the story of how she fell in love with him. She met him on her way to the store to get something to pack in grandpa's mining bucket. Daddy followed her all the way down the railroad tracks to the store and back again. She was almost home when he finally got the nerve to stop her and ask her for her banana, she had in the paper bag. "I'll get a whipping if I give it to ye", mommy said. But he kept on until she gave in. She did get a whipping she said, but she also found herself a husband. They were married right before he left to go to the 3 C's. Daddy use to tease mommy in a loving way but she sometimes took it serious and got mad at him. I will never forget the time he teased her about burning down our toilet. One evening after dark mommy went out to the toilet taking a burning piece of Alden's catalog with her to see her way by. As she left, she threw the burning piece of paper down the toilet hole. Naturally, with all the pages of Alden's Catalog down the hole, it caught on fire. I watched it burn from the window of the back bedroom, as a matter of fact everybody in Crawford came out to watch our toilet burn. I could smell the rotting manure burning as the toilet fell into the hole. Daddy teased mommy, saying she had burnt down the toilet so she would finally get bathroom fixtures put into the house. She swore it was not true, that it was an accident, and I knew daddy was only kidding, but she took it seriously and got mad at him. I thought they were funny. Daddy teased Mommy about being jealous too. He was a handsome man and the twin Bailey girls from up Crawford Mountain walked by the house so daddy would notice them. I think this had pleased daddy, and he laughed about it, but mommy got so mad you could almost see fire burning in her eyes. Then there was also another girl whom, mommy said, had a crush on daddy. She was the daughter of an old man who lived three houses down from us. The old man had the nasty mine disease everybody called "black lung" and could not do much for himself. Daddy would go down there to help his daughter move doc from inside the house to the porch so he could enjoy the day. Mommy said daddy just went down there to see Sheena. Sometimes Daddy would get mad and tell mommy she was being silly, that he was trying to help that old man. Mommy would just shrug her shoulders. She knew not to say too much and get daddy all riled up. Sometimes mommy and daddy would fight. They would scream at each other and mommy would cry, sometimes he would even hit her. Mostly they fought over the grocery bill. Daddy was sometimes cruel, making mommy come up with every penny she had spent that month on groceries. Even though they argued and teased each other, they still worked together to make ends meet.

CHAPTER 20
Mommy's Crochet Dollies

Mommy had made many sets of Crochet Dollies through the years. It helped to bring in a little money to buy our soup beans. Her little finger on her right hand had become crooked from so much crocheting. She made sets of three, one large and two smaller ones, starched them, so the ends stood up like butterfly wings. She put them very carefully in brown paper bags and made us go up and down the roads of Crawford, Bonnyman and Typo selling them to our neighbors for three dollars a set. I often cried when I had to go. It was so embarrassing going to the parents of my classmate's houses trying to sell them crochet dollies. Mommy always said I was being silly when I fussed and made me go anyway. One day, after I had thrown a terrible fit, Annette jumped on me saying I should not have thrown such a fit. She said, mommy wants us to sell a set of dollies so she can get us something to eat for supper. I was still mad, clutching the paper bag of ruffled dollies, wishing I could just throw them in the creek and run away.

Having no luck in Crawford, we walked on into Bonnyman. A cold wind, filled with a whirling mist of snowflakes, had started to blow. We fought against the snow filled wind on into Bonnyman. Annette was determined to sell a set of dollies. We stopped at several houses, but we were not even let inside the door. Finally, one of my classmates, a new girl in school who came from a big city far off, stuck her head outside her door and yelled at us, "Hey Loretta," she said, "you and your sister want to come in and warm up and watch some cartoons on T.V. with me?" Annette wanted to go but I did not, afraid she would ask us what we had in our bags and what we were doing out in this snowstorm. Annette went in, despite my objection, so I followed. The girl, Brenda, and her brother were sitting on the couch. Her brother gave me a strange stare as we came into the living room, like we were not exactly welcome. I stood close to the door ready to make my exit if he said anything nasty to me.

The Store at Blue Diamond

Brenda's Mommy came into the room and said, "Brenda, who are your friends?" I thought she was going to run us off the way mommy often did our friends, but instead she smiled and asked the dreaded question. "What do you girls have in the bags?" Immediately Annette pulled the dollies out to show her. The snowflakes had melted upon the brown paper poke, making the ruffles on the dollies go flat, but she did not seem to notice. She started going on and on about how pretty they were, asking Brenda which ones she thought was the prettiest. Brenda picked a set with a small line of dark blue trimming around the top. We happily went home to give mommy the three dollars. A big smile came over her face where earlier there had been a depressed, worried look.

This made me feel better because I knew I had done something to make her happy. She went off to the store to get some soup beans and a six pack of Pepsi's. She even bought us some candy at Marvin's store. Mommy had sometimes used the money she made from selling Crochet dollies to help daddy pay on the grocery bill. Effie, the store owner's wife, often turned us down when we went to the store to get our paper bag of soup beans and Pepsi's. She would look at us with a prudish, irritated look, a look that pierced into my very soul, and say, "You go home and tell ye mommy that I can't let you'll have any more groceries until Ernest pays me some on this grocery bill." Then she would square her shoulders, lift her head and go behind the cooler, completely ignoring us. I always felt like a no body as we sneaked out the door like scolded dogs. I looked forward to getting my half of Pepsi in the evenings and this really upset me when she turned us down. We faced those cold words from her so many times through the years that it became a dreaded experience to go to the store.

Mommy hated to tell daddy when Effie turned us down for groceries. He would get a strange look on his face, his mouth would turn down, deep wrinkles would come into his forehead and a saddened worried look would come into his eyes. He would drop his head and walk out the door saying very slowly, like the words had choked in his throat, "I'll take care of it Glad".

Through the years there had been many evenings like that. Sometimes it took daddy a couple of days or even a week to get it straightened out with Marvin, Effie's husband. He and daddy had been friends and Marvin tried to give daddy all the breaks he could. He had a much kinder way of telling us about the grocery bill then his wife, Effie, did. He would never turn us down, he would just say, "Tell ye daddy I need to talk to him," and then he would pat us on the head as we walked out the door.

Daddy had spent a lot of time down at Marvin's store. It had not been unusual to see him sitting on boxes of canning jars Marvin had stacked against the long white meat cooler, elbows resting on his propped knee. He usually had a Pepsi in one hand, caught up in deep conversation with Marvin and the other miners in Crawford, and a cigarette in the other. The screen door, with its faded Kerns Bread sign, would make a loud banging sound slamming behind my sisters and me as we came into the store but most of the time daddy had not even noticed we were there. Marvin, a short, hefty man, would be leaning his huge body up against the shelves behind the counter, talking in gasps between sentences because a cigar would be stuck out the corner of his mouth. I liked to look at the things I could not have, things such as doughnuts and store pies and cakes. Finally, I would go to the rusting Coca-Cola cooler, slid the door to the left and stuck my head way down into the musky cool air and reach for my six Pepsis to fill my paper carton. When Marvin would finally notice my sisters and me, he would get a small paper poke to weigh out our lb. of pinto beans and my sisters and I would head back up the road toward home. Sometimes if daddy had noticed us and the grocery bill was not too high, he would send candy home but most of the time he did not.

My sisters and I were tattletales and often told mommy if we saw daddy eating candy bars or drinking Pepsi's down at the store. Mommy would shake her head at him when he got home and I would hear her say, "You shouldn't eat things in front of them youngans if ye ain't going to buy it fer them." I honestly believed he did not really notice we were even there. His mind was still at the mines or out deer hunting with the men.

We had also traded at the store up Crawford mountain at Tarie's store. It was smaller and didn't' have as much as Marvis's but we were sent there when Effie would not let us have our soup beans and Pepsi's. They were not as harsh to us but would only let us have a few things. In the bottom of the store was a church house for the holly rollers. They sang and talked in tongues and could be heard all over Crawford. Their preacher was Brother Ale, and he really knew how to preach a God-fearing sermon. Henry and Omie Tarie were Christians and tried to help us as much as possible but Omie told mommy they had to pay for the stuff and couldn't' afford to let her charge a lot. We owed a large grocery bill the day daddy was killed but Henry said we did not have to pay it. We never heard anything more about the bill.

CHAPTER 21
Gladys, A Coal Miners' Widow

Day after day, that summer of 1965, I watched mommy move about doing only the things she had to do. She had lost the zest for life that I had known her to have even in the worst of times. I remembered how she use to stand at the fence in the yard hanging out clothes as she talked to our neighbor on the other side of the fence, Mrs. Johnson. They would stand at the clothesline and gossip for hours, sometimes until late into the night. Mrs. Johnson's sons and daddy had been good friends. They went fishing and hunting together and most of the time they worked in the same coal mines.

Ottis and Daddy

Otis, the youngest, had never married and I wondered why because he was not much younger than daddy. Once I ask him "hey Otis, why ain't you never got married". He and daddy laughed, and Otis said, "I'm waiting fer you to grow up, squirt." I remember Otis and daddy coming into the yard late in the evening smelling of the woods with squirrel tails hanging out their canvas bags. Mommy and Mrs. Johnson would still be standing at that clothesline or sitting on the porch telling their tall tales. Mrs. Johnson usually did the listening and mommy did the talking. Mommy had always liked to talk about her younger days growing up down in Bonnyman. I had heard her tales repeatedly.

Her daddy, Grandpa Neace, like daddy, had been a coal miner all his life until he had to retire because of breathing problems

Neighbors house, Mrs. Johnson

caused by black lung. Mommy was the oldest of my grandparents' nine children, so a lot of responsibility had been upon her shoulders. She had to get up early every morning to milk the cows and cook breakfast for grandpa before he went to the mines. She had loved going to school, she said, but did not get to go as often as she liked. Grandma kept her home one day a week to do the washing, one day to do the house cleaning and one day to do the ironing. That only left her two days a week to go to school. She took cornbread and buttermilk for her lunch, she said. As soon as she got home in the evenings, she had to go straight to work hoeing out the garden. She said some nights she worked until it got too dark to be able to tell the plants from the weeds. Her teachers had sent her lessons home by her sisters on the days when she could not go to school. She did them and sent them back and managed to go all the way to the third year of high school. Her excuse for making us work hard had been "I had to work hard, and it won't hurt you none either. Mommy liked to talk about the strange things that had happened down in Bonnyman and Typo when she was young. I could just imagine all these tales being true because Bonnyman and Typo had been such a spooky and dreary place. Even when the sun was shining bright in the sky it still seemed to be dark along those narrow, dusty roads. The old camp houses had been spaced extremely far apart and the sound of human voices could be exceedingly rare. Occasionally the lonely sound of a train would pierce the silence. Other than the few camp houses, there had been nothing but kudzu vines and railroad tracks. Mr. Humes saw this the day he came to visit and gave a good description of Bonnyman.

"A land of grim associations, it can be the dreariest and melancholy of places; mists and storms brood over its hills through a greater part of the finest summer; huge precipices of naked stone tower on both sides of winding highways. Go where you will, the charm of the unexpected awaits you around every corner."

Mommy's favorite time to tell her strange tales had been in the dust of the evening. Sitting in the warm summertime darkness the hoot owl's would hoot way off in the woods and the water in the creek would ripple on down the branch as I prepared myself by bending my knees into my chest, wrapping my arms securely around my body, leaning against the porch wall to keep my back protected from whatever could be lurking close by. When daddy had been home, he had enjoyed mommy's tales almost as much as we had. He would act like he did not believe them and sort of laugh at mommy and say, "now Glad" but mommy would swear they were true. Mrs. Johnson and daddy would light up their cigarettes, it being the only light in the pitch blackness except the occasional flickering of the lightning bugs, and silently listen as mommy's voice echoed in the night. She produced one dismal story after the other, sending chill-bumps up my spine. Her favorite had been the story of her and her sister's encounter with the black ball. The story goes like this.

One evening mommy and her sisters, Martha and Beulah, were stumbling up the dark railroad tracks on their return trip from church where they had gone hoping to meet boys. As they got almost to the bend in the railroad tracks, about a fourth mile from the house, they heard strange noises like someone beating a tin can on the rocks. Mommy said she then remembered the horrible tale grandma had told her about the shaft at the bend of the railroad tracks. The shaft had once been the opening of a coal mine where a miner had been trapped and died years back. He had beaten his tin drinking cup against the rocks in the mines to let the people, who were digging for him, know he had still been alive. After days of futile effort to get him out, the knocking stopped. Assuming he had died, the opening was sealed, and it became the miner's grave.

Mommy said they stopped and listened as they made their way down the railroad tracks, afraid to go on, knowing they had to pass that opening of the shaft in order to get home. Dim lines of light streaming from a house across the tracks cast shadows on the overhanging kudzu vines hanging from the cliffs giving the illusion of arms reaching out for them, mommy said. They had walked along briskly, trying to make their steps as quiet as possible in the still night. Suddenly they heard clicking of tin against rock. They slowed down again to listen, but the noise had stopped, so on they went past the enclosed shaft entrance, feeling a cold breeze coming from the cracks in the old boards nailed over the opening of the shaft. Nothing happened until they got around the curve, then they heard it again. Something was coming behind them. It was moving at the same rate as they were. They started walking faster but the faster they walked the faster it came. Now they were running, too terrified to look back. It was making a thump, thump as it rolled down the railroad tracks. Finally, they reached the swinging bridge, crossing over the creek to their house. The bridge creaked and swayed, and the water below moved rapidly by the holes in the bridge as they fought to hold themselves steady. Mommy said she looked over her shoulder to see what this thing looked like, expecting to see the miner, but instead she saw a big black, fiery ball rolling on down the railroad tracks. When they got into the house, their legs wobbling from fatigue and fright, they told grandma what had happened, but grandma just laughed and said, "It's just ye imagination playing tricks on ye."

Mommy had other tales, some of which could raise the hair on a person's head. One, about a haunted house down in Typo, I knew well because I had to pass it every time we traveled to the garden and I had also heard this tale from Grandma Neace. This old camp house had once been occupied by a family of "furriners", from Germany mommy said she believed. They had not been very well accepted in Typo, they could not speak English and had a hard time making people understand them. One night, during a severe rainstorm, the whole family completely disappeared. No one knew what had happened to them. Splattered blood was found all around the house, on the front door, and on the bedroom wardrobe. On the mirror of the wardrobe had been a bloody print of a child's hand. On the front porch there had been a large spot of blood. The family's clothes were still inside the house and everything had been in place like they had just stepped out for a little while. Some people believed they had gotten scared of the people in and around Typo and left. Most people believed that a dog had dragged a dead animal through the house making all the blood, but that still did not explain the bloody prints of the child's hands on the wardrobe.

As the years passed, the house had several occupants, but no one stayed long, saying the house was haunted. It stood empty for several years until grandma's sister, Martha, moved in. She too said the house was haunted. She said the wardrobe in the bedroom made a strange knocking noise and the blood on the porch ran red when it rained. Aunt Martha talked about her haunted house with mommy and Grandma Neace every time she came to visit them. She really believed these "furiners" were killed inside the house and was trying to tell her this. She was obsessed with the idea. Grandma never believed her, but Aunt Martha kept on and on until grandma promised her, she would come to her house the next time it rained to see this phenomenon for themselves.

The smell of rain was very heavy in the air one evening so grandma decided now was the time to go, a necessity for the occurrence according to Aunt Martha. Mommy went along. Sure, enough as the rain came down blood oozed from the dark spot on the porch and a muffled pecking sound was heard from behind the long mirror of the wardrobe door. Aunt Martha opened the door, but nothing was there except her winter coats giving off the odor of mothballs. After this, grandma swore the tale was true and so did mommy.

One story mommy had told I knew to be true because it had been a well-known story in Bonnyman. Mommy had been young when it happened, but she would tell you that she remembered it like it was yesterday. This girl lived up in the woods across the road from Grandma Neace's house. Her death had been brought about by her friendliness. It did not matter how poor, how rich, or what color of skin a person had she treated all people the same, smiling and waving at everyone she saw. She had worked for a doctor up in Hazard and every evening, mommy said, she seen her come up the road from where the taxicab had let her out to go up the hill to her house. One evening she did not come home. For several days she did not come home. People began to ask questions. They wondered why her house had stood empty with no lights in it for several nights. Someone took it to the law, and they came into Bonnyman to ask questions. A woman who lived beside the road where the taxicab usually stopped to let the girl out said she had noticed something very strange the evening she disappeared. A strange man, something you did not see in Bonnyman very often, had been seen walking down the road not long after the taxicab had let the girl out. The police hunted the man down and he confessed to his awful crime. He said she had been very friendly to him, thinking she had liked him, he made a pass at her but she let him know she was not interested, and this made him mad. He then followed her home that evening, killed her, cut her body into pieces and strewed the parts all over the hillside up above her house. Mommy said she watched the law comb the hillside gathering the parts of her body in bags.

I often wondered why Mrs. Johnson had sat on our porch and listened to Mommy's tales repeatedly. Mommy had been a particularly good storyteller. Maybe Mrs. Johnson was lonesome. Her daughter that lived up in Bluediamond did not come to visit her often, she had her own family. Mrs. Johnson was alone most of times in the evenings. Her two sons, Otis and Junior, were like daddy; they were either working in the coal mines, down at Marvin's store or hunting and fishing with somebody in and around Crawford. She had had another daughter, but she had been killed a few years before daddy. I remember the day the man in the black suit came to tell Mrs. Johnson's that her daughter had been killed. I was in the yard making mud pies when a strange car pulled over the bridge into her yard. The man got out and knocked at Mrs. Johnson's screen door. She opened it wide enough to allow him to enter but the man just stood on the steps, said something to her, patted her on the arm and left. Mrs. Johnson stood at the door for a few moments, staring out at the road after his car pulled away, and then slowly closed the door.

I went back to making my pies, until I started noticing people coming and going at Mrs. Johnson's house. I went to tell mommy there was something funny going on next door at Mrs. Johnson's. Mommy went over and came back a little later to tell us that Mrs. Johnson's daughter, Chris, had been killed in a car accident up in Leatherwood. Her daughter and husband, along with their three boys, had gone over one of the hills in their car. One of the boys, Bobby, was hurt very badly but Chris had been killed. All the neighbors sat up through the night with Mrs. Johnson. The yellow beams of light shone from her house into my bedroom window, and I could hear the slamming of her screen door echoing in the quietness of the night as people came and went.

The next day they had Chris's funeral and we over to Mrs. Johnson's house to view Chris's body. The purple lights shined down on the casket sitting up against the wall of Mrs. Johnson's narrow, musty living room and laying there was Chris. She looked just like she was asleep. Death had not taken away her beauty. I remembered how alive and beautiful Chris had been as walked around her mommy's yard. Her long black hair would bounce back and forth with the movement of her thin, feminine body. She had dark skin and always had a warm smile which exposed her pearly white teeth. When she saw us in the yard, she smiled? I wondered how someone so beautiful and nice could just get killed like that. I just knew that beautiful people such as Chris had gone to heaven to be an angel for God.

I missed those evenings on the porch after Mrs. Johnson had moved away to Wisconsin with her youngest daughter, Edith. Her house had sat empty, and it was dark and lonely looking. The weeds had grown up around her toilet and little house where she had kept her tools. Daddy had told her he would watch her house for her in case she decided to come back to the mountains, and he told her she would come back because that is the way it is, you eventually return; at least that is what daddy thought. Daddy's best friend, Otis, and his brother, junior, went with her. They were tired of working in those old coal mines they said and told daddy he should get away from them too. I guess daddy waited too late.

CHAPTER 22
Mrs. Fugate

Mrs. Fugate, our neighbor on the hill, came down to our house almost every day during the months of March, April and May. She would check on mommy to see that we were doing alright. Mommy did not seem to be interested in Mrs. Fugate coming down to our house. She had always been one of my favorite people. I felt bad that mommy did not want to talk to her. She had been genuinely nice to us. She lived up on the hill in a two-story camp house that looked as if it would tumble over the hill onto the road and maybe even on our house. She used to give mommy and daddy canned stuff to help us through the winter. She would yell at us children from her front porch to come up there to get something she had to give us. Usually, it was a jar of pickled corn, and she made the best pickled corn of anybody I knew, even mommy, or a jar of green beans or some jelly. I believe she canned extra stuff in the summer so she could give us some when she thought we were out in the winter. She would always warn us to save her jars.

Sometimes she would give us clothes that had belonged to her daughter Ruth. Ruth wore clothes that were befitting to her beauty, clothes that came from the fancy stores in Hazard. Every woman in Crawford was jealous of Ruth with her high cheekbones, dark curly hair, and a perfect figure. She would sit up on the banisters of her parent's front porch in her peddle-pushers like a model I had seen in the "Millie the Model" comic book. She moved away to Ohio with a man she had married a few years back and Mrs. Fugate had been very lonely. She had no one to talk to but mommy and some of the other neighbors in Crawford. Her husband, Irvin, before he died, had not allowed her to talk to some of the people in Crawford, people like Millie Holland or Millie's neighbor on the hill, the Couches. He said Millie liked to tell too many lies on people and her neighbors packed them for her. Daddy said he was right because Millie did like to gossip. She had come down the road in her floppy hat, frizzy hair sticking out on each side, lipstick on her mouth as red as the roses she grew around her house, and a dress cut so low you could see her wrinkled breasts protruding out the top. Irvin did not like this and neither did most of the neighbors, but mommy said Irvin did not have any right to talk about anyone the way he carried on with his bottle of liquor. I would hear him yell and curse at Mrs. Fugate on the front porch. This always made me so mad because I thought Mrs. Fugate was such a nice person and I was sure she did not deserve to be yelled at. Mommy would say "That old drunken sot ought to be shot for yelling at her like that", but daddy would tell mommy to shut up and that she should not be sticking her nose in other people's business. I was afraid of Irvin. He had come down Crawford road hopping on his wooden leg to stand beside the road in front of our house to catch a taxicab to Hazard so he could get his bottles of liquor. His shimmy pants would dance around his thin, shapeless body and his straight greasy hair would fall over his right mean looking eye as he clicked his cane against the pavement of the road. I often wondered how he lost his leg and I asked mommy and daddy, but they did not seem to know. Most of the time I would hide around the corner of the house until the taxicab pulled up. He would gently pull his peg-leg into the cab behind him and wave at me to let me know he knew I was there.

Daddy laughed at us because we were afraid of Irvin. He said Irvin was really a nice man, but mommy would usually grunt and shrug her shoulders when daddy said this and say, "Ye only like him cause he sharpens ye saws fer ye. He ain't worth the salt that goes in his bread. All he's fit fer is to suck on a liquor bottle."

Irvin died a few years back. He died from pneumonia Mrs. Fugate said, but mommy said "pneumonia, my foot he drank himself to death." Irvin would sit on the porch, drunk as could be, and swear and curse at the wind. Mommy said he was talking to the devil and cursing at God. There had been times I wanted to just go up there and tell him to shut up. Mrs. Fugate said he had sat out on that porch all night one night and got pneumonia. He had been sick for days before he died, and she had tried to get him to go to the doctor, but he would not go. She said she found him in his bed dead. His death was kind of sudden. One day he was sitting up on that porch yelling at us children to get off the road and the next day he was dead.

I thought Mrs. Fugate would have been glad he was dead, but she was not. She mourned him for a long time. She was very lonesome, often asking mommy if us children could come up and stay all night with her. At first mommy would not let us go, but she finally gave in because she felt so sorry for her. I liked staying with her because instead of those lumpy, rag-filled, pee-smelling mattresses on our beds, Mrs. Fugate had those nice soft, clean feather beds. Laying in them would be like—laying on top of a cloud. She always got up in the morning and built a fire in her pot-bellied stove and cooked us some oatmeal before we went home. Mommy was now facing the same kind of sorrow Mrs. Fugate had faced—the death of her husband. She finally stopped coming down to the house so much around the end of May, but I had seen her sitting out on her porch by herself staring down at us as she sang her religious songs. I had missed her visits after she stopped coming down.

There had been many donations of food from everywhere after daddy's death. We had been given so many loaves of bread that we had to get Mrs. Fugate to put some of it in her refrigerator. The United Mine workers had given mommy money to help her out but just until she could start drawing checks from the government, they said. London Clemons, from up in Bluediamond, had told Marvin to let mommy have anything she wanted at the store and to charge it to him. Mommy did because the food people had brought during the wake had started to run out. That is the way we had survived for the month of March. April and some of May. People from around Crawford and in Hazard had done everything they could to help but I knew this would come to an end. I had wondered what we would do if the state did not help us. I felt responsible because I had been the second oldest, especially since mommy seemed to have lost interest in almost everything. I worried and wondered if we would survive without daddy.

CHAPTER 23
Bringing the Truck Home

Girls on Bridge

Mr. Humes wrote "The truck was still parked in the Creech driveway, half filled with odds and ends that he had gathered before he was killed-the broken rear window and bullet holes were still evident, reminders of sudden death. Leatherwood No. 1 is about 40 miles from Bonnyman and Ernest Creech made the round trip daily in his battered, international pickup truck"

In late September they brought daddy's truck home. I was awakened around nine o'clock that morning by the loud grinding of the truck changing gears to come down Crawford Mountain. My mind, being confused from sleep, was thinking daddy was home from the mines. I dressed quickly and darted outside. The truck crossed over the bridge, into the yard and ground to a halt in our yard. It had been a windy day and the first signs of fall had set in. The wind fiercely moved the pines on the mountains surrounding the house and swooped through my thin cotton dress. I sat down on the steps of the front porch and pulled my arms around my body to protect it from the cool morning air. A police officer, not my daddy, had been driving the truck. He seemed to have some difficulty sliding from behind daddy's steering wheel. I could see why when he got out because he was a lot larger than my daddy had been. Daddy was a thin man and he only stood 5'5". The police officer was on the chubby side. His belly hung over his bottom half and his police jacket was not completely closed. He went to the back of the truck bed and lifted out a small box of groceries.' His thin strains of hair stood up in the wind as he walked toward me. A look of pity, a look that I had become so familiar with in the last several months, appeared upon his face. He handed me the box, then took a cigarette from his jacket, cupped it from the wind, and lit it. The cardboard box was damp and wrinkled. In the box was a can of peaches and a package of peppermint sticks. Small spots of dried mud had been splattered on the can and boxes. It was obvious they had been in that truck for a long time. Daddy must have bought these at the company store, I thought. He must have been bringing them home to us the evening he had been killed because I knew these had been the things, he had often brought home and canned peaches had been one of his favorite things. I stood there holding the box in my arms watching the sheriff turn around and get into a police car parked at the top of the road. The car turned around and went back up Crawford road, over the mountain and out of sight. Mommy had been standing at the top of the porch, tears streaming down her face. I walked up the steps and handed her the box of groceries. She took them into the house. I sat back down on the steps, thinking of how that old truck reminded me so much of daddy. It had been hard for me to remember ever seeing that truck without him. I had spent many a summer day letting the hours slowly drift by, watching daddy take piece after piece of junk parts to build that old truck. It was almost as if I could still see his thin body leaning over its hood.

Daddy's Truck

I walked down to the truck, moved back the piece of dirty torn blanket covering its right broken window, and stuck my head inside. There had been a familiar smell inside the truck; dampness of deep earth, the smell that daddy always had. There had been a spider web shatter in the rear window and a small hole below it in the cab. Something dark red, almost black, was splattered upon the floorboard and steering wheel. In the sunken leather seat, where daddy had sat as he made his daily trips to and from the mines, was a large cut with straw sticking from it. This straw had been covered with that black stuff. I could not tell what it was, but I had an idea. I went into the house and brought out Annette, my older sister. She looked at the spots and said, "Ye know what that is, don't ye? We'd better clean that out of there fer mommy sees it." I pulled the straw from deep inside the seat. It was damp and sticky and stuck to the tips of my fingers. I turned my hands over. They were covered with blood. Shock overtook my mind, realizing this had to be daddy's blood on my hands. My heart felt as if it was skipping beats. Tears swelled up from my throat to my eyes. I hurriedly backed out the truck door, somehow catching the sleeve of my dress on the metal horn in the center of the steering wheel. It pulled loose and dangled freely from a black wire. In the hole where the horn had fit had been dried blood. I got sick.

Truck in yard

Why had the sheriff even bothered to bring this truck home, I thought? I just did not understand. Why hadn't he just taken it off to some junkyard to rust away out of our sight just as daddy was turning to dust in his grave at Riverside Cemetery?

CHAPTER 24
The Trial

T he months dragged on through the heat of summer. I felt the heat, heard the usual sounds, frogs croaking in the creek and the whippoorwill echoing their lonely hoots way off in the woods, but in my grief, I let the days slip by without hardly noticing summer was passing. The days had drifted by and I spent my time sailing paper boats down the creek or cutting out the pictures of the beautiful women from the magazines our neighbor had thrown in the creek beside our house. Daddy was not around to tell me to stay out of Laura's garbage and mommy did not care. I kept reading over and over the newspaper clipping from the newspaper I found after Daddy's death. I put it on mommy's dresser, and it laid in the sunshine from the window so long that the black ink had begun to fade. It was dated March 5, 1965,

"A coal miner was shot to death Wednesday as he drove across a picket line at the Leatherwood No. 1 Mine of Bluediamond coal Co. State police said the shot came from the midst of a group of pickets whose identity had not been fully established. Lt. Bill Lykins, District State Police Commander, said at Pikeville the victim was Ernest Creech of Bonnyman, Perry County. Two passengers riding with Creech said gun barrels were sticking out of all vehicles parked by the pickets. He also stated the officers had an earlier report that rock shattered the rear window of Creech's pickup truck as he arrived for work Wednesday morning. The shot that killed him was fired through the same window, Lykins also said. Just the one shot was fired but it penetrated his heart, Lykins said. Creech was the father of nine children."

The first night I read that article I cried and cried. He had been just another news article to be read that day and thrown in the garbage. Day after day I sat alone on the porch staring out into the star filled darkness and daddy's old truck wondering what daddy's last thoughts had been. Did he think of us youngans and Mommy, or did he pray for God to save his soul and take him to heaven? Maybe the pain was too great for him to think of anything or maybe he died before he knew anything.

THE WHEELS OF JUSTICE GRIND
COURT AWARDS $65,000

In mid-July there was a trial. Twelve men were indicted for daddy's murder. It took place in Hyden, the county seat of Leslie County, where he had been killed. The sheriff of Leslie County came to our house early that July morning to take us to Hyden. People were staring at us in sympathy as we walked down the aisle of the noisy, cold courtroom to the front bench to take our seats. Everyone suddenly got incredibly quiet and stood for the entrance of the judge. The court was in session, a man said. This man named Bentley Boggs was the star witness. He testified that he saw Sam Gayheart point a long-barreled rifle at the truck an instant before the shooting. Gayheart's wife later testified that her husband had left his rifle at home the day of the shooting.

THURSDAY, MARCH 18, 1965
SECTION 2—28 PAGES

Miners Win Delay In Trial

Picket-Line Slaying Case Reset In July

By KYLE VANCE
Courier-Journal East Kentucky Bureau

Hyden, Ky.—The trials of 15 men charged with killing a coal miner who crossed their picket line were continued yesterday until July 5.

Leslie Circuit Judge William Dixon granted a defense motion for continuance on the ground that the indictments were returned only a week ago and there had been too little time to prepare a defense.

The motion further stated that commonwealth's Atty. Lester Burns obtained statements from the defendants before they could obtain counsel, and that transcripts of the statements had not been made available to defense attorneys.

Time For Research

Due to the shortage of time, defense has been unable to round up its witnesses, and it hasn't been able to research law books to determine the statutes involved, the motion added.

Ernest Creech, 39, father of nine, was shot in the back March 3 as he drove across a picket line at the Blue Diamond Coal Company's Leatherwood No. 1 mine.

The pickets had held stations at the entrance to the mine property, on the Perry-Leslie County line, for several weeks, for the avowed purpose of renunionizing the mine.

In addition to the 15 charged with murder and conspiracy, Bill Perkins, Hazard, field organizer for the United Mine Workers of America, was charged with banding and confederating to commit a felony.

Bonds ranging from $10,000 to $40,000 each were continued in force. All are free on the bonds.

The jury, six men and six women, one of whom was the mother of one of the defendants, deliberated for less than three minutes. The verdict was "not guilty". That was it. It was all over as far as most people were concerned. I searched my brain, wanting to know who killed my Daddy and what for. I wondered if anyone cared. Mr. Humes wrote in his article, "The Creech slaying was no isolated act; last year the same type of roving picket activity killed Aaron Presell in Grundy County, Tenn., leaving another widow and 10 children. The confessed killer was released as the result of a hung jury. It is not so much that the jurors in this case were pro-union; this is a predominantly non-union area. But the juror who votes a finding of guilty knows that he does so at the peril of his life. As a result, autos and homes continue to be bombed and innocent men continue to be assaulted and intimidated, their only offense being their desire to work in the only trade they knew." Today we look back on trial by ordeal, fire or poison as primitive. The roving goons that took Ernest Creech's life are not in a class with these. Nevertheless, it is the 20th century primitiveness that someday people will look back upon it in wondering disbelief."

12 Charged As Accessories In Killing Of Perry Miner

By KYLE VANCE
Courier-Journal East Kentucky Bureau

HAZARD, Ky.—Twelve men are charged yesterday with taking a hand in the fatal shooting of a coal miner who drove across a picket line Wednesday at Leatherwood, Leslie County.

Nine of the 12 were held in the Leslie County Jail in Hyden on charges of accessories to murder. Three were released on bond.

Ernest Creech, father of nine children, died of a bullet wound in the back suffered as he drove from the Leatherwood No. 1 mine of Blue Diamond Coal Co. State police believe the shot was fired from the midst of about 60 pickets parked in their cars.

State police spent most of Wednesday night and yesterday rounding up suspects from among the men known to have manned the picket lines. Other arrests were anticipated.

Arrested on the accessory charges, State police said, were Boyd Messer, Willie Couch, Eugene Hensley, Jack Childers, Bill Baker, Steve Jones, Grant

Col. 5, back page, this section

Continued from First Page

Baker, Howard Gross, Jimmy Suttles, Worley Robbins, James Baker, and Boyd Couch.

State police here said Hensley, Childers, and Gross made bond but they didn't know the amount.

The charges were brought in Leslie County because Creech and two passengers in his pickup truck had crossed the Perry County line when the shot was fired, apparently from a high-powered rifle.

The pickets, usually numbering 50 to 80 at the Leatherwood operation, dwindled to about 30 yesterday morning. Those who apeared dispersed early in the day, State police said.

Leatherwood No. 1 was formerly operated under a contract with the United Mine Workers of America. It was

closed last year and then reopened as a nonunion mine. Some UMW members kept their jobs, but others refused to work nonunion. The picket lines then were set up by diehard union men.

Says He Isn't Responsible

Some of the picketing activity has been attributed to followers of Berman Gibson, a leader of the roving picket movement of 1962 which led to a series of dynamitings, shootings, and beatings.

Gibson said yesterday in Hazard that he is not responsible in any manner for the Creech shooting, or for the Leatherwood picketing.

"I believe in the hereafter," he said. "I do not want the blood of any man on my mind. What is going on up there (at Leatherwood) I don't know anything about it."

On the way back home, through the back, narrow, curvy roads connecting Leslie and Perry County, Mommy asked the sheriff, "Is there going to be another trial to find out who shot Ernest?" He just kept his stare forward at the road and replied, "I just couldn't tell ye, Mrs. Creech." His words were sharp and stiff. I honestly believed at the time that someday, just as Grandma Neace had said, "things always come to the top just as butter in milk does", that daddy's murder would be solved. I was wrong.

Copied from the original Court Brief.

COURT OF APPEALS OF KENTUCKY
File No. S-150-66

BLUE DIAMOND COAL COMPANY, - -   Appellant,

versus

MRS. GLADYS CREECH, Individually, and as Mother
and Natural Guardian of Annette Creech, Loretta
Creech, Connie Creech, Dianna Creech, Onetta Creech,
Charlene Creech, Deborah Creech, Larry Creech, Terry
Creech, and Ernest Creech, Jr., and
WORKMEN'S COMPENSATION BOARD, Composed of
Frank Goad, Jr., Alvin B. Trigg, E. N. Venters, Joseph
Freeland and A. E. Funk, Jr., - - - - Appellees.

APPEAL FROM PERRY CIRCUIT COURT.
HON. DON A. WARD, JUDGE.

BRIEF FOR APPELLEES.

M. B. FIELDS,
Fuller-Fouts Building,
Hazard, Kentucky,
Attorney for Appellees.

This is to certify that copies of this
Brief have been served on the adverse
party and the Trial Judge pursuant to
RCA 1.260.

_____
Attorney for Appellees.

WESTERFIELD-BONTE CO., INCORPORATED, LOUISVILLE, KY.

STATEMENT OF QUESTION PRESENTED.

Is employee's death compensable under the Workmen's
Compensation Act if said death arose out of a labor dispute
concerning the decedent's work for his employer; and
wherein such death occurred from gunshot emanating from
one of a group of pickets, while said employee was leaving
the premises of the employer after completing his day's
work?

COURT OF APPEALS OF KENTUCKY

File No. S-150-66

BLUE DIAMOND COAL COMPANY, - - *Appellant*,

v.

Mrs. GLADYS CREECH, Individually, and as Mother
and Natural Guardian of Annette Creech,
Loretta Creech, Connie Creech, Dianna Creech,
Onetta Creech, Charlene Creech, Deborah
Creech, Larry Creech, Terry Creech, and
Ernest Creech, Jr., and
WORKMEN'S COMPENSATION BOARD, Composed of
Frank Good, Jr., Alvin B. Trigg, E. N. Ven-
ters, Joseph Freeland and A. E. Funk,
Jr., - - - - - - - *Appellees*.

BRIEF FOR APPELLEES.

May it please the Court:

STATEMENT OF THE CASE.

Recital of facts of the case are essentially as stated
by appellant in its brief.

ARGUMENT.

In this case we submit that Creech's death resulted
from the hazards of his employment.

This is a compensable case on two lines of legal
forensics: (1) The collection of words known as the
"street-risk," and/or "coming and going" rule. (2)

2

"Work-connected assault" rule. Thirdly, here is a
combination of the two. All lead, however, to the in-
escapable fact that Creech's death was work-connected.
To pose the converse; would he have been assaulted
and killed if he had *not* been an employee of Blue
Diamond?

The basic test of the "going and coming" rule as
applied to Creech is whether an employee using a public
highway is subjected to greater risk than is the general
public. The general public is not subjected to the
rancor and malice of a large group of pickets whose
livelihood is being damaged by strikebreakers -
"scabs." The employer, in hiring Creech and working
him despite the labor dispute with the union, either
expressly or impliedly made crossing the picket lines
in getting to and from his work a part of the contract.
The employer even controlled and directed the path
of Creech through the pickets. They blocked the only
other access road onto the public highway before this
fatality. Creech went out onto the road through the
only route left. He was channeled through the pickets.
His only means of "escape" from his work was through
them. And per Carl Boggs (BR, p. 25), he was "on
the State Highway, but still in the camp," when he was
shot. Sergeant Murphy (BR, p. 33) had noticed this
labor unrest existing "several months" before Creech
was killed. The lower road had been blocked about two
months. The company officials knew of this labor
unrest because they had (BR, pp. 37-38) reported
violence to the State Police, and such was directed
against the men *who had to drive* back and forth to

No Tears for Ernest Creech

3

work there. Creech, himself, had reported to Trooper Dees that he had been subjected to violence *on the morning* of his death (BR, p. 29), and the Trooper had investigated it.

This sort of violence and unrest had been going on, the whole record shows, during the entire span of Creech's employment. In order to get to and from his work, to which the employer company invited him and directed him, he was forced to get through these pickets, somehow, day after day. We submit that this situation caused him to be more than ordinarily concerned about his own personal safety and the protection of his means of transportation to and from the job. These hazards were peculiar only to present employees who were working in spite of the threats and violence of the pickets, who happened to be on the State Highway. The general traveling public, other than these employees, were *not* subjected to such hazards. His was a risk connected with and arising out of *his employment*, during that period of time and circumstance. He was hired not only to dig coal but pointedly to get (through these pickets!) to work and get home, in spite of the hazardous circumstance. The fact that he was employed and the pickets were not and the pickets knew this, created the hazard of such employment; not his geographical location when he was shot. With this same knowledge and in the same state of mind, dissatisfied employees could have gone *to his home* and killed him. *Where* he was was not the reason for his death. His death was caused by his working for defendant, Blue Diamond, benefitting them but contrary

4

to the financial interests of the pickets. It was *what he was*—a strikebreaker—in their minds, a "scab."

This is not a pure street-risk case, as such. It is a case wherein, although the nature of the particular job (mining coal) may not entail aggravated risk of assault, the time or place of the employment may be such as to increase that risk. The employment, here, required Creech to travel through dangerous locality (where the pickets were located); the only route (made so by closing off the other route by the employer) that he could follow. The bad feeling, the hatred, of the pickets made the route dangerous to Creech and his fellow-employees. A minion of the employer hired at the expense of the union members who were striving for a new contract. The shot was fired while Creech was on the highway. By the same token, it could have been fired while Creech was still on company property (only 120 feet away) or while he was eating dinner at home, or on his way to a movie. No, this is not a pure street-risk case. He was killed because of his employment for defendant. c.f. Larson, Sec. 11.11(b), p. 135. A hard-working janitor in this writer's building cut through all the words. The question is not "where;" but, rather, "how come" Creech was killed. c.f. Ky., 191 S. W. 2d p. 239, York v. City of Hazard.

Larson discusses this problem exhaustively. Among his remarks are:

Section 8.42, p. 68:

"One could with equal logic say that a person employed as a lion-tamer was exposed to no greater risk of attack by lions than anyone else who hap-

5

pened to be in the cage. It was of the essence of the claimant's peculiar employment that it brought her into the area where the risk of attack *by wild animals* was increased." * * * The court said: "it makes no difference that the exposure was common to all out of door employments in that locality in that kind of weather . . . It was a hazard of the industry."

Section 11.00, p. 131:

"Assaults arise out of the employment either if the risk of assault is increased because of the nature or setting of the work, or if the reason for the assault was a quarrel having its origin in the work. A few jurisdictions deny compensation if the claimant himself was the aggressor; most reject this defense if the employment in fact caused the fight to break out. An increasing number accept the idea that the strain of enforced close contact may in itself provide the necessary work connection. Assaults for private reasons do not arise out of the employment unless, by facilitating an assault which would not otherwise be made, the lunatics, drunks, and children have generally been found to arise out of the employment, and the same has been held by some courts in the case of unexplained or mistaken identity assaults, although there is authority to the contrary."

Section 11.11(b), page 135:

"Similarly, although the nature of the particular job may not entail aggravated risk of assault, the time or place of the employment may be such as to increase that risk. This has been held to be a ground for assault award when the employment required the employee to work in or *travel through a dangerous locality,* or when the employee was required to work at night."

6

Section 11.12, p. 143:

"And injuries in the course of violence due to labor disputes are uniformly held to arise out of the employment, whether a union man is attacked by nonunion men, or nonunion men are attacked by union men."

Section 11.13, p. 146:

"The error in most of the cases denying compensation is the assumption that the sheer passage of time converts a work-connected dispute into a personal one."

Section 15.00, p. 195:

"As to employees having fixed hours and place of work, injuries occurring on the premises while they are going to and from work before or after working hours or at lunch-time are compensable but if the injury occurs off the premises, it is not compensable, subject to several exceptions. Underlying some of these exceptions is the principle that course of employment should extend to any injury which occurred at a point where the employee was within range of dangers associated with the employment."

Section 15.13, p. 199:

"The Commonest ground of extension is that the off-premises point at which the injury occurred lies on the only route, or at least on the normal route, which employees must traverse to reach the plant, and that therefore the special hazards of that route become the hazards of the employment.

"This general idea seems to have been accepted by the majority of jurisdictions in some degree. Two Supreme Court cases, the Parramore case and the Giles case, have lent prestige to this view. In the former, an accident at an intersection of a country road and a railroad 100 feet from the plant was held compensable, because this was the *only* means of access to the plant; and in the latter, the same result was reached when the point in question was on the most convenient, though not the only, route. Two technical limitations on the value of these precedents must be mentioned; first, the narrow point of the holding is that the awarding of compensation under these circumstances does not deprive the employer of property without due process of law; and second, the Utah act, involved in both cases, awards compensation whenever the injury arose out of or in the course of employment."

Section 29.21, p. 452.101:

"There is no single class of cases in which the basic purpose of compensation law have so far miscarried as in these 'delayed-injury' cases. A mere recital of some of the fact situations leading to denials is most eloquent argument that can be made to show that something is wrong with the coverage formula; a watchman was assaulted on his way home by two workmen who had been discharged on the basis of the watchman's report; deceased had discharged an employee, who months later killed deceased out of resentment at the discharge; a bartender who had ejected a drunk from the bar for boisterous conduct was assaulted by the drunk four blocks from the bar; a waitress on her way home was assaulted by a patron whom she had refused to serve an hour earlier; and a self-imagined creditor of the lodge of which deceased was secretary killed deceased while the latter was on the way to work, because of grievance in connection with a debt allegedly owed by the lodge to the assailant.

8

"Sometimes the court has been able to find special circumstances which enable it to surmount the course of employment obstacle. If, for example, the disgruntled employee was considerate enough of the foreman's compensation position to attack him near the plant shortly after the latter left work, instead of the following week-end, the court might find 'continuity of cause . . . combined with continuity in time and space' and award compensation, as Judge Cardozo's opinion did in Field v. Charmette Knitted Fabric Company. Similarly, *in strike cases, an assault near the plant* may be held compensable because within a 'zone of danger' created by the employment. But since the ultimate test applied by Judge Cardozo was whether 'the quarrel from origin to ending must be taken to be one,' *it should make no difference how widely separated the assault was from the employment* in time and space if it remained an inherent part of an employment incident."

It still refines down to the question, "how come" Creech was assaulted and killed? He was killed because he was an employee of defendant. The Corkin case is quite in point in holding:

Ky., 385 S. W. 2d 949, p. 950:

"The theory that an injury must be incidental, or the hazard peculiar to the nature of the employment is fundamentally indistinguishable from the principal of proximate cause, or foreseeability . . .

"We are persuaded that the True case is not sound. It is therefore overruled. We accept the view that causal connection is sufficient if the ex-

9

"Corkin's employment was the reason for his presence at what turned out to be a place of danger, and except for his presence there he would not have been killed. Hence it is our opinion that his death arose out of the employment."

Wherefore, appellant prays the Lower Court judgment be sustained.

Respectfully submitted,

M. B. Fields,
Fuller-Fouts Building,
Hazard, Kentucky,

Attorney for Appellees.

CHAPTER 25
Last Month In Crawford

Mr. Humes wrote "From her Social Security and VA benefits, Gladys Creech must feed, clothe and shelter 10 children, including a four-month-old baby. Adding to her future uncertainty is the fact that the state will soon build a road through her property and she does not know where she will go; of course, she can do nothing about a new place until she receives payment for her present home."

In March of 1966 we moved from Crawford to Airport Gardens. Some of our neighbors had already moved. Mrs. Fugate's son moved to grapevine, and so did the Combs family. The Whites moved to Bonnyman. Mrs. Johnson came from Wisconsin to settle with the road people for her house. She had come over to talk to mommy while she was home. She told mommy how much she had loved daddy and that she was so deeply sorry that he had been killed. Her voice was edged with a sadness that I had only known to come from her when she had lost her own daughter, Chris. Otis had gone over to riverside Cemetery to visit daddy's grave and he gave mommy a picture of daddy and him he had taken one evening after they had come out of the mines. They were still black with coal dust and daddy looked as if he had a mustache.

Mommy had gotten daddy's cousins Woodrow's wife to teach her how to drive so mommy bought a white and light blue 1964 Chevy impala. She then went out house hunting. She looked at several houses and even took us to look at some, but I did not want to move. She settled on a house in Airport Gardens, about three miles from Hazard. It was close to the river. I remembered the year of 1963, looking out over airport gardens from atop of Crawford Mountain as the flood waters washed over it. Daddy had been at our sides, standing in the rain, staring down over the mountain in disbelief. I remember that awful smell of the river and how it penetrated the air. I did not really think that was a good place to move to. I felt I had been so lucky to have been living on top of Crawford Mountain at the time of the flood and I just did not understand why she wanted to move down there.

Mommy would drive us to the A&P store in Hazard to get groceries. We would just go through the store and pick up everything we wanted to eat. I discovered things such as cottage cheese and olives, things I never knew existed. I should have been happy, but I was not. All those years of dreaming of store-bought things I now had I would have given back for those days with daddy, to be back in that garden spot digging in that hot scorching earth or seeing him down at Marvin's store sitting against that meat cooler drinking a Pepsi and eating a moon pie.

Mrs. Carter, Blue Diamond's cook had died. They found her dead in her toilet, had a heart-attack they said. I was shocked. Was everybody I had known and admired going to die. I had seen her freshly covered grave at Riverside Cemetery when we stopped to visit daddy's grave. She was buried close to daddy and I was glad because I knew I could visit her grave when I went to visit his. In March 0f 1966 we moved from Crawford to the new house in Airport Gardens. We took mommy and daddy's cast iron bed, their wardrobe and the cedar chest which contained daddy's clothes. In the chest she had packed his mining cap, mining belt, his bee helmet, his penny loafers she had been sewing the day they came to tell her he was dead and the rest of his clothes, a brown leather jacket and a fancy pair of dress pants he had worn when he had gone to Ohio to look for work in the factory years back.

Grandpa Neace and Uncle James and Jennis came bright and early that morning to load grandpa's big wooden bottom truck up with our things. Uncle James drove daddy's old cream-colored truck to Airport Gardens. We loaded it as full as we could. This gray, ghostly mass of concrete blocks looked cold and empty as I climbed into the back of daddy's truck. Its great gapping windows were like sad eyes staring at me, its door like a mouth open wide crying "don't leave me, please don't leave me". This house had been the last thing left of my daddy, this house he had built with his own hands. Soon the house and most of Crawford would to be covered over with the mountainsides that I had awakened to every morning for sixteen years. The life that I had known was completely gone. We would be moving to a place where there was no place to raise a garden, have honeybees, or raise hogs. It was a subdivision about 6 miles out of Hazard at the bottom of Crawford Mountain. We would live off the checks the government would provide and the money the coal company had given mommy. My goal the year of 66 was to finish school and do as I had told him that I would do the night I sat at that kitchen table staring into his sad blue eyes. It was as if his spirit had been in that house staring back at me as we faded over Crawford mountain. I said a silent good-by to all that was left of our life with daddy. The year of 1965 had passed into history and the man that was Ernest would just be a memory to most people. The last few paragraphs of Mr. Humes article really summed that up.

Airport Gardens

"If Ernest Creech had been a beatnik, peacenik, or "freedom fighter" super heading a mob demonstration bent on stopping a construction project or storming an army embarkation pier, you can bet your last depreciating dollar that his killing would have evoked an impassioned New York Times editorial calling for the dispatching of federal troops to Leatherwood.

His cause would have been fought tooth and nail by the American civil liberties union, the Americans for democratic action and the national council of churches we would quickly hear form the usual list of Jewish rabbis, Protestants and catholic divines and fellow traveling professors as they signed their names to full page ads in his behalf.

Daddy's Grave

Talkative moralizers on the subject of civil rights like Hubert Humphrey and Walter Reuther would dispatch telegrams to the bereaved family and the voice of America would be telling Ghana and Indonesia that Ernest Creech was "killed by hate" of the type of "Dallas hate" that killed President Kennedy: CBS would send its crack TV crews to film the "shame of Kentucky" and Huntley and Brinkley and Ralph McGill would sermonize on the "cancer of racism" that infects the south. But Ernest Creech was nobody: nobody. That is. He wasn't even a communist or a northern civil rights agitator or a left-wing professor calling for a Viet Cong victory over American troops, thus the big silence. Maybe we have entered an era wherein this is simply the way it has got to be. But if so, let us not fool ourselves about the nature of the change and the depth of the tragedy.

Creek that ran in front of our house

Bridge

Mommy standing in rubble of our house

Sitting on grave

Mom at home today

In Bonnyman, Kentucky life goes on. The voice is still, but the magic of Ernest Creech's personality lives on.

Sixteen

Looking fresh as mountain

Air as moon beams danced across her hair,

Crickets sing their lonely song; a shy young girl stands all alone,

Autumn leaves crush beneath bare feet,

in age old mountains that seem to sleep.

The autumn winds begin to blow in hollows deep

where no man goes,

A little girl wanders on and listens for a starlight song.

The sound of rushing waters near, the little girl cries a tear,

The moon goes slowly behind a cloud, a little girl sits, full of fear.

She lays her head down by a tree

and dreams sweet dreams of what could be.

The birds wake up and sing their song

but the little girl had already gone.

The mountains reach up to the sky

and in deep dark hollows voices whisper good-bye.

I, **Loretta**, at the age of 16.

This was a picture taken of me in 1967, my first summer at Alice Lloyd college in Pippa Passes, Ky. There I spent my first two years of college and it was here that I wrote most of my book to heal myself of the sorrow of losing my daddy. Alice Lloyd was only a two-year college at the time; we still wore the white sailor-type uniforms, were not allowed to associate with the boys and lived under the strict rules of the woman who had founded the college, Alice Lloyd. It was a lonely time for me, but I took solace in writing stories in my notebook, stories from and about my mother and daddy and our life before and after his death. In 2005 I decided to put them into a book. I am not a writer, only a story- teller as my mother was. I have tried to write this book in that manner.

References

"No Tears for Ernest Creech"
by Mr. Ted Humes. Human Events, November 13th, 1965

"Miner Fatally Shot Crossing Picket Line"
Courier-Journal East Kentucky Bureau, 1965

Printed in the USA
CPSIA information can be obtained
at www.ICGtesting.com
LVHW010100270124
769490LV00080B/3031

9 781959 165873